READ BETWEEN MY LINES

Read Between My Lines
The Musical and Life Journey of Stevie Nicks

Copyright © 2006 by Sandra Kathleen Halliburton

Cover and book design: 1106 Design
Distribution by Midpoint Trade Books

READ BETWEEN MY LINES

THE MUSICAL AND LIFE JOURNEY OF STEVIE NICKS

Sandra Halliburton

To

Laura for believing in me and being my soul mate

Nancy for listening to my colliding thoughts and always making me feel like family

Helen for helping me see what's possible

Stevie whose life and lyrics inspired me to fulfill my dreams

With Love

Acknowledgements

The book began about three years ago after seeing the 1997 Fleetwood Mac reunion DVD, *The Dance*. Having lost track of the band for many years while building a career in management consulting, I was impressed by their presence and sound. In particular, I hadn't seen Stevie Nicks for years, other than in the Admiral's Club at LAX sometime in the '90s, and was quite intrigued. I began to research what had happened to Stevie, having remembered her drug dependency in the '80s and seeing that she had overcome some major challenges. Looking for something to recharge me after years of business travel, I found inspiration in her triumphs. Stevie's passion for "giving back" through her many benefit concert performances also served as inspiration and was instrumental in my decision to write this book.

It was Laura Archer who really encouraged me to write the book. I had been threatening to write "I am not a Widget" in honor of a former employer, but never had the passion or time to do it. Once becoming mired in the music of Stevie and Lindsey Buckingham's forty-year relationship, however, I was hooked and no longer lacked the passion to write my book.

A very special thanks to Laura, Nancy Willett, Linda Delaney, and Heidi Youngkin for going to the concerts with me and to Jim and Helen Jancik for escorting us to Chastain Park in Atlanta. I am also grateful for my long-time friend, Sallie Willett Shea, who feels like family just as all the Willetts do including Olin who shares a birthday with Ms. Nicks! She,

Laura, Linda, Nancy and Rosanne Hart all read early iterations of the book and gave me the inspiration to finish.

I would like to honor the late Bob Simmons, a very special friend whose courageous three-year journey with cancer was a testimony to the strength of his faith. He never lost hope. Even when gravely ill, he shared his radiant smile with everyone around him while giving sincere encouragement and love. Such a wonderful man.

Thanks to Elizabeth Jeffett Norman, a wonderful friend and business colleague, Helen and Warren Jacques entered my life last year. What an incredible and precious gift they have been. The Jacques make the world a happier place and truly imbue the meaning of love, warmth and friendship. Thank you Helen for proofreading and for being my fashion and design consultant!

It was Janet Wilson, my friend and former professor, who really got me started in publishing. Thank you Janet for being such a special force in my life. I have learned so much from you.

I sincerely appreciate the warmth and loyalty Gerry Kroloff, Executive Administrator, Arizona Heart Foundation, has for Stevie and her family. Thank you Gerry for sharing your passion for heart disease research and your appreciation of Stevie's contributions.

To John Kinney, web master of Stevie's official site (*www.nicksfix.com*) for his guidance, Hudson Turner for assisting with research and Natalie Giboney of *FreelancePermissions.com* for such professional handling of requests. I am very grateful to have Elizabeth Bashara (Bashara Concepts) taking care of publicity. Thank you Rosanne for the introduction several years ago. A special appreciation also goes to my friend and neighbor, Sarah Reed, (Hilary Hudges Design) for designing and developing my initial web site and to Bruce Moilan for helping me design and launch the permanent site. Thank you to photographer, David Lawrence, makeup artist Kim Rozell and stylist Charla Romo for bringing out the best in me during our photo shoot for the book's cover picture. Who knew that could be fun! It was also a pleasure working with Michele DeFilippo of 1106 Design in Phoenix who designed the cover and completed the book layout.

To all the photographers including: Janet Mayer, Tiffany Sledzianowski, Chris Walter, Henry Diltz, Lynn Goldsmith, Bettman, Barbara Kinney, Roger Ressmeyer, Trapper Frank, Scott Weiner, Mandy Gossett, Philippe Carly, Bill Paustenbach, Sam Emerson, Neil Zlozower, Debbi Radford, Melissa Loukas, Barry Brecheisen, Ron Galella, B. King, Mazur, Ray Sette, Maryellen Suter, Kathy Uhlenbrock, Willie Jennings, and Thom Westhof.

Many thanks to Gail Kump and all the Midpoint Trade Books team for believing in this book.

Table of Contents

Introduction

Creative, intense, generous, and amazingly resilient, Stevie Nicks's legacy may well be her vision of introspective folk rock as a legitimate genre. Whether as a member of Fleetwood Mac or as a solo artist, she has mesmerized audiences for more than thirty years. Female musicians of today often credit her with being a force in paving the way for women in rock 'n' roll. Stevie has made mentoring a major part of her life. She tells young artists her story so that it may save them from making some of the same mistakes. Stevie's life story, with all its highs and lows, provides us an opportunity, regardless of our musical and artistic talent, to grow from her tremendous strength, persistence, and courage, while learning from the many challenges she has faced.

In honor of Stevie Nicks's intriguing and endless musical and personal accomplishments, *Read Between My Lines: The Musical and Life Journey of Stevie Nicks* portrays key events in this musician's life and shows how pain, separation, loss, and love influenced the writing of her autobiographical and poetic lyrics. Extensive research on her life and analysis of her songwriting provide an interesting look inside her soul but not "unless she lets you." On "Stand Back" from *The Wild Heart*, Stevie's second solo album, she wrote, "No one knows how I feel…what I say unless you read between my lines." Her highly personal songwriting tells the story. After completing a thirty-day treatment program for a cocaine addiction that lasted almost a decade, Stevie told us about her experience in "Welcome to the Room…Sara" released on Fleetwood Mac's *Tango in the Night* album. Sara is her muse and the name she assumed while undergoing rehabilitation.

As adults, we tend to seek chaos and unhealthy patterns of behavior in an attempt to meet those needs that we feel were not met during our youth. The late John Rosen, a prominent psychiatrist from Pennsylvania, in coining the phrase "seek the mother you know," was referring to our unhealthy choices and to the degree of pain we allow those decisions to generate in our lives. What caused Stevie Nicks to be drawn to the emotional turmoil and physical harm she endured and, indeed, helped to create for a decade and beyond? One contributor may well be the trauma and loneliness she experienced as a result of frequent family moves in her childhood, which happened due to her father's successful business career. But we will never really know. We can be sure, however, that her painful life experiences have generated some of the most prolific songs ever written. Early on, Stevie was forced to mobilize her tremendous personal strength and innate survival mechanisms. Who knew these skills would be used over and over as she built her musical dynasty while enduring the pain of unrequited love, personal loss, drug addiction, depression, and chronic fatigue syndrome?

It was Mabel Normand, a silent movie comedienne, whose life most closely paralleled Stevie's. Plagued by illness and misfortune, she too was independent-minded and inexplicably eccentric. Poignantly, they share the ability to possess and foster subtle "girl power" while maintaining an unexplainable kind and gentle manner. She wore elaborate clothing and hats and was also quite generous. Not unlike Stevie, Mabel, for all her times of unhappiness, frequently tried to keep a cheery outlook and smile even though inside she was being emotionally and physically eaten up. She was often described as being silly and light-headed just like a five year old. While her bearing could be stiff and her movements relatively restrained, she at times, in her expressions, showed a certain sophisticated savvy. The two artists also share a strong sense of humor, a sudden marriage of convenience and what some might call an isolated and lonely life.

True to her generosity and passion, Stevie's multiple benefit concerts in support of heart disease research at the Arizona Heart Foundation demonstrate how she has used her fame for purely philanthropic contributions. In fact, she and her family have been one of the Foundation's major contributors. As a result, restricted funds were used to construct the Arizona Heart Foundation's (state-of-the-art) Cardiovascular Research and Education Building which will be dedicated to the Nicks family and begin operations in the summer of 2006. Funds originally allocated for the center were then used for ground-breaking research into the transplantation of muscle cells from the leg to the heart, thus improving cardiovascular function. The procedure is being tested in human clinical trials with success. Jess Nicks, Stevie's late father, became Chairman Emeritus of the Arizona Heart Foundation Board of Trustees after serving as the Foundation's chairman for three decades. "A large number of people in my family have died of heart disease. My wife and I both have it and are worried about our children continuing the disease pattern," said Jess Nicks. "We've come a long way in the last 20 years in heart disease research, but not far enough. Hopefully this building will escalate the research process and bring forward the elimination of heart disease." Gerry Kroloff, Executive Administrator of the Arizona Heart Foundation worked for Jess for many years and has described him as "everybody's mentor." Inspired by the trauma of heart disease in her own family, Stevie has devoted herself to this serious medical mission. By listening to the title song "Trouble in Shangri-La" from her 2001 solo album, one can hear the ambivalence Stevie associates with fame and fortune, as she imparts the message that one can achieve success without knowing how to handle it. "I realized that whenever you get to Shangri-La, there is always going to be a lot of trouble. There just is," Stevie has said. "If you make it to paradise, there's going to be a lot of trouble surrounding you, and people have a lot of trouble staying there because of that. People make it to the top of their field and think that that's paradise, and it isn't somehow."[1]

During their discussion for *Interview* magazine, Sheryl Crow asked Stevie the meaning of "Trouble in Shangri-La." "That song was written during the last two months of the OJ Simpson trial, but that's not what it was about," she told Sheryl. "What the OJ trial made me aware of was relationships and how difficult they are—especially for people who are in the public eye and are very famous—and how difficult it is for them to hold on to Shangri-La. Of course, to somebody who doesn't make very much money and would just love to live in Shangri-La, it's hard to even hear that. But there is a price to pay for this kind of fame. It's strange, because in a sense I was writing about the same things when I recorded *Bella Donna*, almost twenty years ago."

Blessed with a privileged lifestyle as the daughter of loving parents Jess and Barbara Nicks, Stevie chose a direction in her life that would for many years give them cause to worry. First, they worried when she was a starving waitress and cleaning homes while living with her longtime lover, friend, and partner in song arrangement, Lindsey Buckingham. During the following years, the painful and never-ending breakup with Lindsey, her own physical exhaustion, and her long-term recreational and prescription-drug addictions kept her parents concerned for their highly successful yet tormented oldest child.

Stevie kept them in the dark until her excesses and painful experiences had reached unmistakable proportions. In 1983, Jess Nicks was asked if he and Barbara worried how success might have changed their daughter since it so often leads to hedonistic excess, wild parties, and constant drug-taking. Though he was sure it hadn't, Stevie was in fact already mired in the midst of her nine-year cocaine addiction, spending vast amounts of money and partying noon to night. Jess went on to say, "We watch her success, of course, and stay very close to her...but we don't really think about her as anything other than our little girl."[2]

Stevie spent much of her time touring and was rarely home, yet her father often took the role of tour promoter and really wasn't so very far away. Nevertheless, as many parents are, hers were in denial. They simply couldn't believe their little girl was dealing with more than she could handle. One cannot even fathom how difficult this must have been for them. Stevie has expressed, in many ways, how much she loves and appreciates them for always being there for her.

If one recognizes her mantra, "I feel always that I want to live up to my end of the bargain, that I was given something by God, and He asks only that I give Him back something"[3]—it's easy to understand why Stevie is so driven. Certainly, she has given (and continues to give) her heart and soul in all that she does, but not without pain and personal sacrifice. Stevie, with age and wisdom, has come to terms with some of her pain and with her unhealthy behavioral patterns as demonstrated, perhaps subconsciously, in lyrics from "Running Through the Garden," the eleventh cut on Fleetwood Mac's latest album, *Say You Will*, released in 2003. In her lyrics, one can draw parallels to many of Stevie's life events—the last several months of her cocaine addition, her tumultuous relationship with Lindsey Buckingham, or even her realization that her addiction to Klonopin (the drug she was prescribed to ease withdrawal after her cocaine cessation), had wreaked havoc on her creativity and made her indifferent, reclusive, overweight, and unhappy. Knowing as much as we do about her sometimes challenging and painful past, it was heartwarming when she candidly admitted after the Fleetwood Mac reunion tour, "We didn't all enjoy it very much the first time because we were too high and too uptight, so this time it's really been fun."[4]

An endearing creature with more endurance than most, Stevie has contributed to the fantasy world of many—men and women, both straight and gay—while maintaining the same surprisingly out-of-style chiffon-and-lace image. When Steve Morse of the *Boston Globe* asked Stevie in 1991 if she leaves the house wearing her trademark platform boots, she said. "Heck, yeah. It's no act. I wear the ones with six-inch heels, in every color. I have them all handmade. I wear the shawls and the boots to the grocery store, and people trip out. They look at me like I'm from outer space, and I know they're thinking, 'Well, it's really her.'"

Without question one of the most recognizable and highly regarded figures in the history of rock 'n' roll, Stevie is anything but typical.

One

The Formative Years

Stephanie Lynn Nicks, arguably rock 'n' roll's most notorious singer and songwriter, was born on May 26, 1948, at Good Samaritan Hospital in Phoenix, Arizona. "I could not pronounce the word 'Stephanie' when I was little. My pronunciation of it came out as 'TeeDee,' which was [eventually] turned into Stevie. My mother still calls me TeeDee." Stevie gave this account in response to a question posed at her official web site, The Nicks Fix (*www.nicksfix.com*). Always true to her fans, she answers questions online in an "Ask Stevie" forum. Stevie elaborated further, "My mother calls me TD Bird. She calls me TD Bird…it's really sickening, isn't it! I was never called Stephanie. My Dad named me Stephanie to call me Stephanie, because he loved that name, so somehow whatever fate just twisted it away and I became Stevie."[1]

It was her grandfather, AJ Nicks, a struggling country singer with German ancestry who first recognized Stevie's performing talent. At the age of four, she began singing duets with him and even performed at a local tavern owned by her parents. He paid her fifty cents to practice her talents. Stevie has credited her grandfather with the start of her musical career. "It would go all the way back to when I was in fourth grade and my grandfather brought home a trunk load of 45s. He and I sat on the floor in my bedroom and listened to song after song after song. That, really, is when I started singing."[2] He even wanted to take Stevie on the road with him but, as any good parents would, Stevie's intervened. Her grandfather's frequent absence from her life because of her parents' decision to keep her home proved very painful for her and most likely led to her future poetry and lyrics reflecting feelings of separation and loss.

As Stevie explained for *Interview* magazine, she would have more than enough opportunity to experience life on the road. "My granddad was a country and western singer, and he left his family and took freight trains and traveled all over, playing in bars and supporting himself by playing pool. So my mom and dad thought, 'Well, there she goes. She's gonna walk down the same road as her grandfather.' And luckily I became a bit more successful than he was."

Stevie's mom has always instilled a sense of responsibility in her. "My mother's mom and dad were divorced very early, and her stepfather worked in a coal mine in Ajo, Arizona, and died of tuberculosis. She had a hard life, was very poor, was 19 when she got married, and had me at 20. My dad went after a big job in a big company, got it, did very well, and liked to move around and travel a lot. My mom got used to it and had a lot of fun, but she's much more practical, frugal—she still sniffs her nose at my dad's and my expensive tastes—and she wanted more than anything else for her daughter and son [Christopher] to be independent and self-assured."[3] Jess Nicks achieved great success in his career as Chairman of Armour & Company and Executive Vice President at Greyhound Corporation.

Despite their early reticence over her destined career in music, Stevie's parents gave her their unwavering support through all the years of her success and hardship. Her father introduced his daughter during the 1982 HBO presentation of her first solo album tour, *White Wing Dove*. Sweetly, fifteen years later she dedicated "Landslide" to her father on *The Dance* reunion tour DVD. Family dedications are not unusual for Stevie. Her fourth solo album, *The Other Side of the Mirror*, was dedicated to her grandmother, and 1994's *Street Angel* honored Stevie's niece, Jessica James Nicks.

This is not to say that she has not woven her mother and brother Chris into her famed musical web. Stevie proudly gave her mother the rights to the song "Silver Springs," a gesture she extended despite her parent's resistance to accept money from their highly successful daughter. Chris manages her merchandizing, and his wife Lori is a long-time friend and backup singer. Jessica Nicks got her first hands-on exposure to rock 'n' roll when she and Fleetwood Mac bassist John McVie's daughter sang the fading bridge to "Say You Will," the title cut on Fleetwood Mac's latest studio album released in 2003. In fact, Chris, Lori, and their daughter, Jessica, share Stevie's Paradise Valley home along with Sara Belladonna and Sulamith India Grace, her precious Yorkshire Terriers.

In 1998, Stevie was able to publicly share the bond with her grandfather when she released "It's Late" (a favorite song of his and one she'd been singing since the fourth grade) on the three-CD box set *The Enchanted Works of Stevie Nicks*. Her first solo album, *Bella Donna*, was a tribute to AJ and all his children, the man who gave her inspiration and got her started. AJ Nicks passed away before Stevie reached her potential, though he knew she would.

As a young child, Stevie was taken by the world of fantasy and wonder, something her mother instilled in her. This love of performing and escape eventually evolved into a career that would launch her forever into the limelight. After seeing the *Stevie Nicks and Friends* concert at America West Arena in 2000, an adoring fan wrote, "One thing I love about Stevie's concerts is that they're some of the very few times where women can transport themselves back into childhood and play 'dress-up' in their own little fantasy world. I wish we had more opportunities to do this!" Stevie's impact on her fans and her willingness to share her passions is remarkable.

Long before women of all ages were wearing flowing chiffon and colorful shawls in honor of their hero, Stephanie Nicks was twirling around in her room with a cape, mimicking the nuns at St. Mary of the Wasatch Catholic High School in Utah. Similarly, before she demonstrated her baton-twirling skills for the University of Southern California marching band and ultimately for the world in the *Tusk* video, Stephanie Nicks was teaching her long-time childhood friend, Karen Thornhill, how to twirl a baton at Wasatch Junior High School. "Even in the early '60s, it was evident. She was just born with this gift. Writing lyrics…poetry. I don't remember her ever without a pen in her hand," Thornhill said in an interview with the *Deseret Morning News*.

Though Stevie lived in Utah just a little over two years, she and Thornhill formed a lifelong bond. It was a painful good-bye for the best friends when Stevie moved to Arcadia, California. "We sat on the curb and cried and vowed to stay close and together," Thornhill continued. That childhood promise was kept, and Karen has routinely visited Stevie in California for many years. Thornhill and her husband were even invited to tour with her childhood friend for a few shows, experiencing firsthand the life of a rock star. "Even though my best friend is a rock icon, she is still just Stevie. She is very sweet, very mellow. She is so genuine. She once told me, 'Don't ever envy my life and not be appreciative of what you have.' She was born with a gift and she chose to follow that star. She gave her all to do this."

Stevie's first song was "I've Loved and I've Lost," a profound title, given what was yet to come. "I wrote my first song on my sixteenth birthday. I finished that song hysterically crying, and I was hooked."[4] She remembers singing it in her high school assembly.

She further elaborated on her first masterpiece for Stephen Bishop's *Songs in the Rough*. "A month before I turned 16, my mom and dad said I could take guitar lessons. They really didn't know if I was going to like it or not, so they rented me a little guitar, and hired a Spanish classical guitar player, and I took six weeks of guitar lessons, twice a week. And this teacher decided he was going to go to Spain to study, and I loved his guitar so much that they bought it from him for me, for probably a thousand dollars. It was a Goya, a classical guitar; it was very tiny. I still have it. I sat down and wrote a song. It was pretty goofy, but it had a chorus and two verses and it had an end. And from that second onwards, I knew I wanted to be a songwriter."

A year later in 1965 while attending Arcadia High School near Los Angeles, Stevie joined Changing Times, a band heavily influenced by the harmonies of the Mamas and the Papas and known as a tribute band to

Bob Dylan. During most of her childhood, Stevie and her family moved throughout the Southwest. Her father's career took them from Arizona to New Mexico, to Texas, to Utah, and finally to California. She has said it was important for her to be flexible.

"I did make friends. I just didn't have time to make too many. So I was very adaptable, I learned to make friends quickly and to get accepted quickly because I didn't have enough time to waste. To be snooty for 6 months until I decided to come down to earth and be a part of everything didn't work at all. So, I just had to be real amiable and friendly and open to people, or, I would be alone for a year and then we would move." For *Interview* magazine, Sheryl Crow asked her what she was like in school. "We moved a lot, so I was always the new girl. I knew that I wasn't gonna have too much time to make friends, so I made friends quickly, and I adjusted really well, and when I'd say, 'I'm gonna miss my room,' my mom would always say, 'There's always a better house.'

"In tenth grade I was at Arcadia High School, in California, which was a very hotsie-totsie school, very cliquey and a lot of rich people went there. And I always dressed kinda crazy and I always had a big straw bag 'cause I wanted to carry everything with me, and so I was kind of odd. I was always kind of in the popular group, but I was also in the not really popular group. I'm sure that if you talk to people that went to school with me, they would say, 'Well, she was a little crazy, she loved her music, and she was interesting.' I think I was very interesting to everybody."

Stevie's father remembered a fond memory from her high school years. "The occasion was a father-daughter night in which he and Stevie performed to a recording of "King of the Road."

"I was singing away, and Stevie was singing away," he said between howls of laughter. "Well, she gets to laughing, and I get to laughing, and I'll be damned if she didn't wet her pants—right there on stage!"[5]

"I got the giggles during the first line, 'Trailer for sale or rent,' and I was just hysterical," Stevie remembered with amusement. "And we had actually practiced this! We practiced for a week! But he kept on singing—he's got a really good voice—and he would give me this look like, 'How could you do this to me?'"[6]

It was in 1966 that her family moved to Atherton, California, where she attended Menlo-Atherton High School. During her senior year, Stevie met Lindsey Buckingham, an event that would forever change her life. Stevie spoke with *The Source* about meeting Lindsey. "I was a senior in high school and Lindsey was a junior. And we went to a Young Life meeting, which was a religious meeting that simply got you out of the house on Wednesday nights. He was there and I was there and we sat down and played 'California Dreaming.' I thought he was darling. I didn't see him again for two years and he called me up and asked if I wanted to be in a band." By the summer of 1967, Stevie and Lindsey had joined Fritz, or, more formally, the Fritz Rabyne Memorial Band, named after an unsuspecting student in their school.

Stevie's family moved again in 1968 to Chicago, but this time Stevie chose to stay in California. Upon graduating from high school, Stevie attended San Jose State University. Just before she was about to receive a degree in speech communication, she dropped out. She had planned to become an English teacher, but she instead walked away from the school to pursue her musical career with her Fritz bandmates. The band opened for acts such as Janis Joplin, Jefferson Airplane, Santana, Creedence Clearwater Revival, and Jimi Hendrix. Most influential for Stevie was watching Janis Joplin. She has said you couldn't have pried her away with a million dollar check. It was then that she learned a lot of what she does onstage. She wanted to create the same kind of feeling that Janis Joplin had with her audience. Other admitted influences include The Everly Brothers, Jimi Hendrix, Joni Mitchell, Bob Dylan, and Grace Slick. As noted by Tim Rigney, "there also seems to be some parallels between Stevie's highly personal and emotional songwriting and early Fleetwood Mac writers. Songs such as 'The Ghost' by Bob Welch and 'Man of the World' by Peter Green certainly seem to have underlying similarities to some of Stevie's work."

As Fritz's manager was unsuccessfully attempting to secure a record deal, the male members of the group were beginning to feel threatened by all the attention their petite female singer was receiving. Stevie learned another life lesson from this situation. "Those guys didn't take me seriously at all. I was just a girl singer and they hated the fact that I got a lot of the credit. They would kill themselves practicing for ten hours and people would call up and say, 'We want to book that band with the little brownish-blondish-haired girl.' There was always just really weird things going on between us. I could never figure out why I stayed in that band. Now I know it was in preparation for Fleetwood Mac."[7]

Although the band called it quits in 1971, Lindsey and Stevie remained musically connected and soon began an intense romantic relationship. After they'd moved to Los Angeles to pursue their musical dreams, Keith Olsen helped them land a record deal with Polydor Records in 1973 and produced the *Buckingham Nicks* album. Keith has summed up the music phenomenon they possess quite well. "There was a timber that happened when the two voices would join that was unique. You never heard that before. I don't think you've heard it since. Those two voices sing like that and sound like that for a reason. They were meant to sing together."[8]

Stevie once explained the *Buckingham Nicks* opportunity for Ian "Molly" Meldrum of ABC Australia. "They only took me because they knew that they weren't gonna get Lindsey without me and also as a little kind of back up to Lindsey, so we signed the *Buckingham Nicks* contract and we did an album that is now ours, actually Lindsey and I bought it, and we may just go back in and remix a little bit and maybe do a little singing on it and because, I sat in a room with Lindsey for nine months, in his father's coffee plant, a little tiny room while we did half of the songs on that record on a four track. Like we'd go when the workers went home. We'd go at seven o'clock and we'd stay until six-thirty all night long, up by the Cow Palace in San Francisco and I would sit there every night, all night long and listen to him like put the lead on *So Afraid* or the seven minute acoustical version of 'Frozen Love' which he just plays all the way through."

Although Stevie still waited tables while Lindsey stayed home to perfect his music, they continued to write songs for the album. Stevie remembered spending her last $111 on a beautiful white blouse to wear for the cover shoot. Instead, she and Lindsey both appeared on the album bare-chested. She was reportedly crying when they took that picture. Lindsey was mad at her; he thought she was just being a child and didn't understand they were creating art! Stevie recalled that doing the nude cover was "the most terrifying moment of my entire life."[9]

Provocative cover or not, the album wasn't successful, and Nicks and Buckingham once again fell on hard financial times. They moved in with friend Richard Dashut, whom they'd met while making their album. Stevie managed to pay the bills by working as a waitress at a local restaurant named Clementine's, working for $1.50 an hour. "We were so poor that we used to share a hamburger for dinner, or sometimes a slice of pizza," she told Charley Walters for *Headliners: Fleetwood Mac*. Record producer Keith Olsen would pay Stevie $250 per month to clean his home. "When Stevie would come to my door and say, 'Okay, I'm gonna clean it,' she looked just like Carol Burnett. It was absolutely hilarious."[10]

Dashut has remained a key figure in their lives and would go on to earn the respect and deep friendship of the members of Fleetwood Mac as a co-producer of every Fleetwood Mac studio album from 1977 to 1987, as well as the 1995 release of *Time*, an album in which Stevie did not participate. When the *Buckingham Nicks* album was unsuccessful, Stevie and Lindsey felt the world had ended. They had recorded in a large studio and were proud of their record. When it was dropped by the record company, they felt as though they were back to square one again.

"It was two years of solid depression," Stevie told *Creem* magazine. "It was hard when you practice that hard and you sound that good and everybody tells you that you should be doing something else. You want to say, 'Well obviously we're not from the same planet, because I didn't sit with this guy for five years and sing like this for you to tell me that nothing we do is commercial. You're crazy.' It was a terrible time. Because Lindsey and I just couldn't understand how we could sit down and sing a beautiful song to you and nobody liked it—and it was so pretty it made me cry. It was like, we don't belong here, nobody understands us." Oddly enough, the *Buckingham Nicks* album achieved cult-status in Birmingham, Alabama! Prior to joining Fleetwood Mac in rehearsals, Lindsey and Stevie played their last concert as a duo for a sold-out crowd of 6,000 Alabamians.

Stevie's parents were growing tired of seeing their daughter unhappy and waiting tables. "My dad said, if you're going to do it, be the best, write the best, sing the best and believe in it and yourself. And as long as I didn't give up on that, it would be OK. It was great to have supportive parents, though I'm sure they really would have been much happier at one point if I'd done something else, because they didn't think I was strong enough. I was always sick and Lindsey and I had no money and whenever they'd see me, I'd be really down. My relationship with Lindsey was tumultuous and passionate and wild and we were always fighting, so I was never happy."[11] Her parents encouraged her to set boundaries on how long she would continue working toward launching her musical career. She vividly remembers being without money while she was waiting tables. She would get money from her parents once in a while, but they would have supported her financially if she had wanted to move home and go back to school. She chose to continue doing her own thing in LA, and thus had to get by without their help.

Heeding her parent's request, Stevie ultimately decided to give the rock 'n' roll gig six more months before going back to school or changing the direction of her career. As fate would have it, it wasn't long before Stevie and Lindsey received the phone call that would forever change their lives. The caller was Mick Fleetwood of Fleetwood Mac, a successful English blues band. The band needed a new guitarist. Mick, having heard the *Buckingham Nicks* record in a studio he'd visited, was impressed with Lindsey's hard-earned guitar skills.

Lindsey and Stevie have been asked about their Fleetwood Mac fate many times. Lindsey shared his recollection with the *Ventura County Edition*. "Well, let's see…I think Mick Fleetwood was looking for a recording studio. Stevie and I had just finished an album, and Keith Olsen, our engineer, put something on tape to show his work as an engineer. It turned out to be our song 'Frozen Love' which had a searing guitar solo. At that time, Stevie and I just happened to be in the back room, and when we walked in, there was this really tall guy stomping his feet to our song. Bob Welch was leaving the band, so Mick Fleetwood asked me to join. At first, he didn't want both of us, but I told him we were sort of a package deal."

What an understatement that turned out to be!

School picture
(*Source:* ScottsdaleLife
July / August 2000)

Stevie with her lollipop
(*Source:* ScottsdaleLife
July / August 2000)

Stevie with her mom in 1973
(*Source:* Scottsdale Life, *July / August 2000*)

Two

Stevie and Lindsey: An Enduring Phenomenon

Without question, the most influential force shaping Stevie Nicks's haunt-
ing and insightful musical art form continues to be her forty-year relationship with Lindsey Buckingham. More recently, as we watched Stevie
on the *Say You Will* tour, we could only imagine what it felt like to be back
on stage performing with Fleetwood Mac's most intriguing cast of characters, excluding Christine McVie, who was working on a solo career and
had chosen to retire from the rock 'n' roll touring lifestyle.

Looking back on Stevie's introduction to the rock 'n' roll experience,
once things got rolling it all happened very quickly. Stevie described meeting Lindsey a little differently for *Spin* magazine. "We had gone to some
party and he was sitting in the middle of this gorgeous living room playing a song. I walked over and stood next to him, and the song was
'California Dreaming,' and I just started singing with him. And so I just
threw in my Michelle Phillips harmony, and…he was so beautiful. And
then I didn't really see him again until two years later, when he called me
and asked me if I wanted to be in his rock 'n' roll band, which I didn't even

know existed. And within two or three months we were opening for Jimi Hendrix, Janis Joplin, all the San Francisco bands. Two years later, we packed up and moved to Los Angeles with about twelve demos."

Though their relationship began on a musical level, it would change soon after the breakup of Fritz. When they migrated to Los Angeles without their Fritz bandmates and were pegged by the Polydor label for the *Buckingham Nicks* album, excitement abounded—but not without the reticent pain of leaving friends behind. In Nicks's room at the Tropicana Motel, the foundation for the fiery romantic relationship began when innocence was lost. "Why it happened between me and Lindsey was because we were so sad that we had to tell the three guys in the band that nobody wanted them, only us."[1]

"I think there was always something between me and Lindsey," she told *Rolling Stone*, "but nobody in that band [Fritz] really wanted me as their girlfriend because I was just too ambitious for them. But they didn't want anybody else to have me either. If anyone else in the band started spending any time with me, the other three would literally pick that person apart. To the death. They all thought I was in it for the attention. After the breakup of the band we started spending a lot of time together working out songs. We started spending all our time together and…it just happened."

Lindsey has produced some of Stevie's most successful music over the years. While he has not always seen the expectation that he develop her songs as fair given their tumultuous relationship, he did recognize their inherent partnership. "Whatever her music was, I mean, I was always this soul mate who knew exactly what to do with it."[2]

Despite the record deal and ultimate explosion into fame as Fleetwood Mac's newest additions, Lindsey and Stevie found themselves dealing with the competitive and possessive characteristics as lovers and bandmates. "Rich and famous or starving and poor, we went through the same problems. He always wanted me to himself, but somebody had to go out and earn some money. All he wanted to do was play his music. When I came home I'd always get a slight cold shoulder. He wouldn't quite trust me about where I'd been or what I'd been doing. When we broke up, two years after joining Fleetwood Mac, it was like a living nightmare…everything about me seemed to bug him. My laughter, the way I could deal with a lot of difficult things, all made him want to cringe. So I changed when I was around him. I became mouse-like and would never dare offer a suggestion."[3]

Deciding which of Stevie's songs would be part of a Fleetwood Mac record often created major turmoil as Stevie expressed for *USA Today*. "Lindsey would say, 'I don't want this song on the record,' and I'd say, 'I hate you!' and I'd be out the door and at home making up speeches I wanted to deliver to him the next day. Then it would get worse." When he wanted to, Lindsey could often mold her songs into hits. "He could take my songs and do what I would do if I had musical talent. When he wasn't angry with me, that is. That's why there's seven or eight great songs, and there's 50 more where he wasn't happy with me and didn't help me."[4]

On whether Lindsey is a perfectionist, Stevie had this to say to Molly Meldrum at ABC Australia. "Utter. To the point of, why can't you just come and play? And it's like, 'Well I can't just do that.' And that's the reason, and I love Lindsey, but that's the reason that Lindsey and I aren't together. It's because I'm radical, you know, its like, I just want to play, I just want us all together here, and set up some microphones, and a camera and I just want to play. And Lindsey, it needs to be perfect for Lindsey and so his perfection drives me crazy because I think he doesn't have any fun, and my radicalness drives him crazy because he thinks I'm not as good as I should be."

In between Fleetwood Mac's first and second album with Lindsey and Stevie on board, things began to unravel for all the couples in the band. Not only were Stevie and Lindsey having major issues, Christine and John McVie also called it quits. Even Mick Fleetwood's marriage was showing signs of dysfunction. Given his intense commitment to the band, he had little time for a home life. Stevie has described the breakup with Lindsey as a gradual process. "I don't even remember what the issues were; I just got to the point where I wanted to be by myself. It just wasn't good anymore, wasn't fun anymore, wasn't good for either of us anymore. I'm just the one who stopped it…In Sausalito, up at the little condominium. Lindsey and I were still enough together that he would come up there and sleep every once in a while. And we had a terrible fight. I don't remember what about, but I remember him walking out and me saying, 'You take the car with all the stuff, and I'm flying back.' That was the end of the first two months of the recording of *Rumours*."[5]

Stevie cited yet another source of tension and pain within the band. "I remember getting very upset with Lindsey one night when I realized that he and Christine [McVie] had written "World Turning." I had been with Lindsey all those years and we had never written a song together. Plus, I walked into the studio and they were singing it together."[6]

Lindsey Buckingham's interpretation was a bit different. "It's been very much a series of situations, of having to adapt. The kind of role that, say, Stevie and I had towards each other and that I had in *Buckingham Nicks* as compared to what happened six months after we joined Fleetwood Mac—I really had to turn around. It was a very good thing to happen. I gained so much more appreciation for Stevie that way. I had to reevaluate the whole thing. There's been a lot of adapting to do."[7] He further elaborated during a BBC Radio interview. "Stevie and I, even when we were lovers, we never were really best friends. We've always competed…ever since we started going together back in 1971. [There was always] tension on a musical level…even though we were excellent lovers, we were competitors as well."

Stevie and Lindsey were in agreement regarding the competition. "I don't think there's ever been a competitive element between any members except for Lindsey and me, and that started way before Fleetwood Mac and goes right on to this day and will go on till we die. That's just the way we are—Mr. and Mrs. Intense."[8]

Even as Stevie and Lindsey embarked on their solo careers, the competition continued. "I love Lindsey. I love him very, very much and I wanted Lindsey to make it and I wanted this album to be successful. If this album is more successful than my album, I would be so glad. You know, when "Trouble" (the single from Buckingham's LP) came out, I was saying, let it go straight to the top. Because it only makes my life easier when Lindsey is happy. 'Cause when Lindsey is happy, he's really in a good humor and he's wonderful and he and I really get along and we're close. For me, when you love somebody, you want them to be the best."[9]

When speaking with Dan Neer and James Fahey on *Reflections from the Other Side of the Mirror,* Stevie described the making of *Rumours* as a "horrifying experience." She explained that with three couples on the rocks for twelve months, everyone got into other people's stuff. They were all giving advice, constantly upset and sarcastic, and getting up and slamming doors. It just kept happening. No one was ever calm. They were constantly uptight and worried. She described the experience as hell but confessed the coolest thing in the world was getting through it without disappearing, having a heart attack, or killing somebody.

Despite the turmoil and breakups, the band went on to record *Rumours,* one of the most successful albums ever produced. The ongoing soap opera gave fuel to many lyrics that have been played on radio stations across the world for many years. Lindsey's hit, "Go Your Own Way," is a perfect example. By way of acting out, Lindsey added the vocals at a Sunset Strip recording studio in Los Angeles, describing Stevie's behavior as "packing up, shacking up (with different men) was all she wanted to do." Typical on all Fleetwood Mac songs, Stevie dutifully added the harmony vocals. "I very, very much resented him telling the world that 'packing up, shacking up' with different men was all I wanted to do. He knew this wasn't true. It was just an angry thing that he said. Every time those words would come out onstage, I wanted to go over and kill him. He knew it, so he really pushed my buttons through that. It was like, 'I'll make you suffer for leaving me.' And I did."[10]

"Oh it bugged me terrible. And I had to listen to it every night and sing along with it. It would just put me back in the place where Lindsey and I were when he wrote that song…back to our apartment [where he was] really angry with me. It was kind of like I had to revisit the world of the big fight every time he sang it."[11] With time, Stevie saw the situation more rationally in a BBC Radio 2 special. "Lindsey writes "Go Your Own Way" and I write "Dreams!" I write philosophically, he writes angry! So yes, a lot of the stuff that, you know, little sentences or stuff that he would say would upset me! However, as a songwriter, I have to respect that he's gonna write about what's happening to him, and so am I."

Stevie had her turn at displaying her anger publicly as she remembered during the taping of *Classic Albums: Rumours*. "I wrote "Silver Springs" about Lindsey. We were in Maryland somewhere driving under a freeway sign that said Silver Spring, Maryland. And I loved the name. Silver Springs sounded like a pretty fabulous place to me. And, 'You could be my silver springs…' that's just a whole symbolic thing of what you could have been to me."

"I'm so angry with you. You will listen to me on the radio for the rest of your life, and it will bug you. I hope it bugs you."[12] A bold statement from Stevie summing up why she wrote "Silver Springs," the B-side release for Lindsey's "Go Your Own Way." This onstage battle generated tremendous public interest in a band known for fighting, drugging, and loving. Stevie has found herself reflecting on the Lindsey/Stevie phenomenon during interviews since their arrival in Fleetwood Mac. "Splitting up has not been an easy thing for either Lindsey or me. I think we both knew deep down that it was the only thing we could do. We weren't creating, either of us…It's much better now."[13]

Lindsey found it difficult to control his anger as a result of the breakup. Her success as crowd favorite didn't help either. In March of 1980 during the *Tusk* tour, Lindsey lost it. He was suffering the pain of their relationship and drinking too much. The band was playing a concert in Auckland, New Zealand. Lindsey pulled his jacket over his head and began to twirl in imitation of Stevie during their performance of "Rhiannon." He then ran across the stage and kicked her. Stevie has said he even threw his guitar at her but she moved out of the way just in time. Back in the dressing room, the band went after him. It was Christine who slapped him, poured a glass of wine on him, and told him he'd better never do that to this band again, ever! Lindsey, in an interview with *Mojo* magazine, referred to the incident. "Stevie and I could never quite find each other after *Tusk*. You have to understand that this is someone I met when I was 16. I was completely devastated when she took off. And yet, trying to rise above that professionally, I produced hits for her, I had to do a lot of things for her that I really didn't want to do. If I kicked her onstage, that was…something coming through the veneer. There has been a lot of darkness."

Lindsey considered their relationship a marriage. He was still very young and accustomed to having what he wanted. It wasn't until Lindsey had children that he could be unselfishly dedicated to anything but his music. "When he and I split up in the very beginning, Lindsey was never quite able to understand what had happened to us, and that in itself had to make day-to-day living very difficult for him, and it did for me."[14]

The pair continued to work together in the same band until 1987 but not without tension. "Let's put it this way, we hardly spoke," Stevie told *Microsoft Music Central* in 1997. "We would get on and off the same plane without interacting at all. It's not like that now. Even if Lindsey and I were to totally fall in love again, get married, and get divorced, we would never let it go to that negative place again. We're just too wise now. It got so bad between us that we couldn't even talk. We couldn't communicate. We couldn't work anything out because we couldn't even sit down for five minutes together."

Lindsey admitted to acting out in other ways. "What I do remember, is a show where I purposely sang much of the set out of tune. We got off-stage, and everyone was irate, obviously. They were talking about firing me and getting Clapton. Very well founded, because it was not a professional thing to do."[15]

When Fleetwood Mac's *Mirage* was released in 1982, Lindsey continued to struggle as Stevie's solo album went straight to number one and escalated her more and more in the public eye. He even began to criticize her songwriting, describing her songs as a "little flaky" in an interview with *The Record*. He went on to say, "There's obviously something about her material that people relate to. She's always been a little hard for me to take seriously, because I appreciate a beat, having been weaned on Elvis, and Little Richard and Chuck Berry." Nevertheless, Lindsey does realize Stevie's talent. "There's something emotional that gets through though," he said. "And her voice is so recognizable. I've been listening to Stevie sing for years and years, and when you're that close to it, it's easy to overlook certain aspects of anything."

One cannot listen to Stevie's many love songs without becoming ensconced in her insatiable and tumultuous romance with Lindsey Buckingham. Their public love, pain, separation, and loss are as heart-wrenching for us as for them. Interestingly, her songs often express the importance of keeping feelings intact and alive. But while keeping histori-cal feelings alive can be positive, it can also keep one mired in the relent-less pain of what cannot be. It's intriguing to think about what could have been, particularly when listing to songs such as "Destiny Rules" from Fleetwood Mac's *Say You Will* CD that demonstrate Stevie's nostalgic and unrelenting passion.

While she has acknowledged that "Destiny Rules" is about her relation-ship with Lindsey, only Stevie really knows to whom she is singing when she writes and performs her other raw, heartfelt songs. With her audience in mind, Stevie told *Borders.com*: "I write from a specific experience and make it as general as I can so it will be able to reach out and be understood by a lot of people." After seeing Janis Joplin, she would search to find the same connection with her audiences. Stevie has always believed she was sent here to take people away for a while and make them happy. Clearly, she has achieved her goal.

Although Lindsey is married, Stevie does have a connection to his chil-dren and has carved out a place in his life that is only for her. If we could truly understand the pain they experienced while creating the *Rumours* album in that dark and reclusive studio in Sausalito and how many drugs it took to make it through all the painful years of touring and conflict, we might realize that their separate lives are probably for the best. It may be hard for some to understand how, after many years of reciprocal abuse, the couple has formed a very close friendship despite years of not speaking. It seems that we are often most connected to those who are with us during our painful journey to maturity.

In 1990, Stevie offered a brilliant metaphor for her relationship with Lindsey. "He and I were about as compatible as a boa constrictor and a rat. But we've had our final words. We will never be able to work together again, ever even speak again, which is very sad. In any relationship you come down to a point where you say things that you can never take back, and we've said them. It breaks my heart."[16] While it is widely known that the fight Stevie and Lindsey had in 1987 when he chose to leave the band rather than participate in the already-booked *Tango in the Night* tour was embellished in Mick's autobiography, *Fleetwood, My Life and Adventures in Fleetwood Mac*, it was nevertheless one of their worst battles ever. Lindsey's last words before storming out after the altercation, were, "Get that woman out of my life—the schizophrenic bitch!"[17]

Christine has said that Stevie did not deal well with Lindsey moving on and dating other women. Stevie confirmed her pain in an *Off the Record* radio interview. "To break up with somebody and see them the next morning in the hotel breakfast room...possibly with another person...uh...was about as difficult a situation as you could possibly imagine. And for me to walk into a...to the breakfast room and see Lindsey sitting with a girl...I mean it was an instant U-turn in the first place...and uh, I mean it was—it was enough to make me absolutely ill."

An interesting exchange between Lindsey and Stevie occurred as a result of a *Dallas Morning News* interview. Both parties were interviewed at separate times for an article that appeared on April 2, 1993. Stevie started the ultimate dialogue with, "Lindsey and I had been going together from about 1971 to 1976. But we never really broke up until that moment [his leaving in 1987]." Upon hearing Stevie's comment, a perplexed Lindsey proclaimed, "Oh, really. Did she say that? That surprises me. She went through quite a number of men, ah. I'm surprised to hear that actually. That's very interesting..." It really is quite telling that even in 1993, seventeen years after their breakup, Lindsey would react so cynically and with such apparent interest to Stevie's remarks. It goes to show, just as he has stated in interviews and song lyrics over the years, Lindsey still didn't understand what happened to them.

Despite their current reconciliatory behavior, years went by when the couple never spoke. "I cooked and cleaned and took care of him. I mean, my mom and dad considered Lindsey and I married. So did I. So did he. Now Lindsey and I don't speak at all...It's a sad way to end a long, wonderful relationship."[18] The silence continued, as she explained for *The Island Ear*. "Currently, Lindsey and I have no relationship...Basically, I

think Lindsey and I had sung our last song. We had taken that relationship as far as it could go without one of us killing the other. Plus, he had
treated me so badly for so long. I'd walk into a room and he'd become the
most sarcastic, unpleasant man on the face of the earth. I have total
respect for him [as an artist]. I don't know if he has any for me. He feels I
broke up our team. So, for that, in his mind, I should be tortured for days
and then killed."

In 1994, Stevie continued to express a cynical view of their fate. "I
haven't talked to him since the [Bill Clinton] inauguration. We're really
not friends. We're really not anything. We did not break up friends, and we
have never been friends since. He is not really able to have any kind of a
relationship with me. I just bug him to death. Everything I do is abrasive
to him. He's scary when he gets mad."[19]

With the opportunity to see Lindsey for Clinton's inauguration in 1993
came a series of connections for the former lovers. Eventually in 1997,
Stevie and Lindsey, along with the full *Rumours* line up, were on tour promoting the release of *The Dance*. "Now on the road, we've had many really
good talks," Lindsey told *Mojo* magazine. "We've known each other most
of our lives and yet we're still trying to figure out what's going on.
Obviously, a lot of love as a subtext. But where is that love? How do we get
in touch with any of that? For all of us, the decisions we make now are
going to determine how we are as people until we die. Stevie and I are trying to look at it…with care."

After many years of harbored anger and unresolved issues, Stevie and
Lindsey were finally given an opportunity to connect on a level that
appears to make them both happier—while also building the trust that
was lost so many years ago. "Lindsey deals with me on a much kinder
level. And I'm more willing to be open with him. It's nice to think I might
go to my grave being Lindsey's friend and not a thorn in his side for all
eternity."[20]

Stevie and Lindsey (even while releasing songs about each other for
their 2003 *Say You Will* album) are still working through the pain. "Now I
just adore him," Nicks told *Mojo*. "He is my love. My first love and my love
for all time. But we can't ever be together. He has a lovely wife, Kristen,

who I really like, and they are expecting their third child. The way he is with his children just knocks me out. I look at him now and just go, Oh, Stevie, you made a mistake! But when we go onstage together we are able to experience our love affair again—and again and again! For two and a half hours, four times a week. There isn't really anybody in my life—it wouldn't be good for me now anyway, I'm always away. But when hard times come over the next twenty or thirty years, when people we love die, he'll be the first person I'll call. Knowing that now, I think he has been able to let go of all the nasty things that happened and realize that, like I said to him, Lindsey, you'll always have me. I'm always a phone call away. So you get it all."

Should we feel sad that Stevie has not settled into an intimate relationship with someone else? Regardless, Stevie has evolved and knows what makes her happy. And she is going for it. When she decided the songs she'd submitted for the *Say You Will* CD did not meet her own expectations, Stevie asked for thirty days in Phoenix to write new ones. Spirit catcher in tow, she arrived in the fall of 2001 at the rental house in Los Angeles where *VH1* was capturing the making of *Say You Will* in reality-TV fashion (later aired as the *Fleetwood Mac: Destiny Rules* documentary and now available on DVD). She had returned with a cassette demo, and, by the time he'd heard the fourth song, Lindsey was in tears. Years of pain and sorrow were alleviated as they jointly arranged and sang those songs.

As the pair worked on the arrangement of Stevie's song, "Thrown Down" for the *Say You Will* album at their LA rental home, *VH1's Destiny Rules* portrayed them discussing the lyrics. The song, admittedly, was written to demonstrate her feelings for her first love. They exemplify her complicated and often strained relationship with Lindsey.

Stevie told him, "I'm talking to you," when he cautiously explained that she'd changed person tense, a violation of the rules of writing. When watching the *VH1* special, one can feel the tension as they worked on the song, evidence that their often competitive and explosive relationship is still very much intact. Lindsey tried to be tactful as he challenged her person tense issue and suggested she change "Now you're going home" to "Now he's going home." Stevie held her own, saying he wouldn't be questioning Bob

Dylan about *his* lyrics! "That is how I write." Her self-esteem abounding, she told him he couldn't change it because it was so beautiful.

Stevie's fans are fanatical and evidently thrilled to see her back on tour with Fleetwood Mac, despite her inability to hit the high notes on songs like "Rhiannon" after all the cocaine, Kools, and vocal abuse. Indeed, many think she is singing better than ever.

Similarly, she now tends to keep her popular onstage antics to a minimum. It's not easy twirling and doing high kicks in platform shoes at her age. She often wears black high-top Reeboks rather than her vintage platform boots. In fact, certain songs had to be retired during the tour as they were just too hard on her voice.

Lindsey's niece, Cory Buckingham, has said that for Stevie's birthday in 2004, she was presented with a dark chocolate cake covered in gravestones—one for each of her retired songs. Given how much she sees her songs as children, there may have been a time when Stevie wouldn't have found humor in that little prank, especially since her birthday fell during the week of the *Say You Will* tour with dates that had to be cancelled due to problems with her voice. She took it all in fun. Even Christine McVie used to scoff at the idea that Stevie thought all her songs were her children and since she was the mad songwriter, she had tons of them!

However, her animated nature during the *Say You Will* tour portrayed the emotional roller coaster of Fleetwood Mac's mantra. On "Landslide" she was touchingly sentimental. Lindsey played acoustic guitar as they gazed into each other's eyes, and they ended the song in an embrace. Alternatively, her performances on "Gold Dust Woman" and "Stand Back" were vintage Stevie, filled with the energy of her early solo career. It was like reliving the *Live at Red Rocks* concert in the eighties, but without all the cocaine.

Lindsey walked onstage with her hand in his as he'd done so many times before, and Mick escorted her off at the end of the performance. Despite her alleged stage fright and the shot of tequila she downed just before coming onstage, her confidence was refreshing. Though she appeared slightly stilted and awkward during the first few songs of the set, she once confided in an interview with *Encore* that "I walk on stage, I'm very strong, I'm still pretty cute—and I rock."

Upon reaching the stage, Mick Fleetwood had the beat as they launched into "The Chain," the jam-session-turned-song filled with classic Fleetwood Mac harmony. It would seem that Stevie's infamous lyric, "If you don't love me now, you will never love me again" was written to immortalize the love/hate relationship she'd had with Lindsey. It has since come to represent the "unbroken chain" of Fleetwood Mac.

Stevie with Lindsey Buckingham—mid '70s
(Source: www.nicksfix.com)

Three

The Beginning—Fleetwood Mac (1970s)

After hearing the *Buckingham Nicks* album at Sound City and recognizing Lindsey Buckingham's guitar savvy, Mick Fleetwood gained consensus from the band that he was the one to replace Bob Welch, Fleetwood Mac's fourth guitarist casualty. Knowing that Lindsey came with a female singer/songwriter, he ensured Christine McVie was okay with the addition of another woman to the Fleetwood Mac family. There was a point when Mick wanted only Lindsey, and Stevie never really forgave him for temporarily treating her as an afterthought. Regardless, Mick does recognize her immense value to the band and believes she has an extremely powerful aura.

When Mick and the band officially extended the offer, Lindsey Buckingham and Stevie Nicks didn't need to think about it very long. Stevie's perspective was one of musical contribution and survival. She felt they could add something to the band. Moreover, she believed they should join for the simple reason they might otherwise perish from lack of food!

As Stevie remembered for Molly Meldrum of ABC Australia, they weren't even asked to audition. "The reason I told you we lived on Orangegrove and Fairfax was because Christine's mother was very psychic and the last thing that Chris's mom said to her before she died was 'you will find it on Orangegrove' and of course Christine with her dry English humour is sure she's going to be picking oranges somewhere in an orange grove in California, and they found us on Orangegrove."

"From the day that we all met at a Mexican restaurant and they drove up in these 2 wild Cadillacs, white like with the fins, clunked up! Lindsey and I are like going these people are strange and they get out and it was really like love at first sight, how could you not love these people? So we had dinner, and it was never like 'do you want to join the band?' It was like 'well rehearsal's tomorrow at 5pm in the basement and you'll get paid $200 a week in cash for each of you,' and I'm going 'we're rich! We're rich.'"

It was not an easy transition for Stevie. "We were a strange group of three English people and two American people, and that was very hard on the road, because we were just so different. Christine McVie had Steve Winwood carrying her books home from school, and Eric Clapton was best friends with Mick Fleetwood when they were sixteen, and I could not even relate to that. It was like, 'You guys are too famous for me. And I'm getting really nervous.'"[1]

"Without Mick's offer," she told *Circus* magazine, "I think we would have had some really terrible problems. We were nothing, with no money and suddenly we were making two hundred dollars a week each. I moved into a more expensive apartment. Lindsey moved in with me two weeks later. We'd been trying to break up, off and on, for years." Luckily, Stevie had learned responsibility prior to joining Fleetwood Mac. "I worked at the Copper Penny, Clementine's and Bob's Big Boy. I supported Lindsey and I for years, 'cause he never worked or had a job. I was pretty grown up when I joined Fleetwood Mac. I was glad, because I would not have been able to handle that kind of overnight success. From the day that we joined to June of that summer, we were famous."[2]

They booked studio time at Sound City and after ten days of rehearsals recorded the material. *Fleetwood Mac* was released in July of

1975, followed by a thirty-five-city tour. The first single, Christine McVie's "Over My Head," was released in July, backed by Lindsey's ballad, "I'm So Afraid.", with famously intense guitar solos. Initial reviews were, at times, harsh on Stevie, describing her singing as callow and raucous in comparison to Christine's golden-throated voice. Naturally, she took the reviews hard and was prepared to leave the band. The success of "Over My Head," Christine's upbeat song with Stevie harmonizing, helped curb her fears. But it was the "Rhiannon" phenomenon that finally put to rest any ideas of leaving.

The second single was, in fact, Stevie's "Rhiannon," released in January of 1976. It rapidly surpassed "Over My Head," reaching number eleven on the charts. In September the album's third single, Christine's "Say You Love Me," also climbed the charts. By the summer of 1976, *Fleetwood Mac* had become the largest-selling album Warner Brothers Records had ever released.

Though the two women had competing songs on the charts, they developed a very close friendship. Stevie looked up to Christine, feeling she provided a sense of stability and strength for her. The mystical and bohemian image Stevie created was quite the opposite of Christine's stoic British nature. Christine was happy to stay behind her keyboards.

In 1987, Christine described her relationship with Stevie. "We're not competitive. What's pulled us through over the years is our ability to share some bloody good laughs. Stevie is always, always, always working on songs and insists on blasting you to smithereens with a massive sound system she brings wherever she goes. She's the poet of the group, without question. Though she owns a home in Phoenix, she's a nomadic gypsy who, it seems, has lived in practically every house in Hollywood. She just gathers up her favorite things and rents some place. She surrounds herself with an entourage of friends, whereas I enjoy my solitude. I'm very domesticated and deeply entrenched in my house with its rose garden and picket fence—my little patch of England in Beverly Hills."[3]

"Chris will tell you that there were times in the last six or seven years when she was a little jealous. And I swear to God I never knew. She never let me know. Never one comment to the effect of 'I could really have done without you.' I'm sure there were times when I'm flying around the stage in my gossamer chiffon where she had to think to herself, 'Wow, what's this? Fairy school?' And never once did she make me feel like that. Because she knew from the beginning that I was real sensitive and that I love her so much that anything she'd say to me would cut like a knife. So she was always very careful."[4]

In an interview for *Goldmine*, Christine was asked to define the difference between her and Stevie. She openly stated, "Stevie was always a lot more visible. She has this sort of personality which is conducive to that. She enjoys all the accolades, she enjoys the attention, she's at the front of the stage, she adorns herself in stuff, she does it and commands a lot more attention than someone like myself, that has always been, or tends to have been back with John and Mick as a rhythm person in the band."

Stevie has taken the opportunity to share her feelings as well. "Christine and I have been through so much together we're way past certain things like arguing. We just sit down and discuss. If I was upset, she's one of the people I'd call. She'd never be too busy to take me to her house. In the beginning, Chris helped me not to get upset when everybody was upset with me. I've never been able to show up anywhere on time and have almost caused the band to miss concerts. Without Chris, I don't think I'd have liked going on the road as much. Chris and I have never been one of the guys. We always demand respect and get it. We're quite a pair."[5]

Stevie further elaborated for *Creem* what it was like when she first joined Fleetwood Mac. "They made me feel wonderful. I fell madly in love with all of them immediately, and even though I knew in my heart that they didn't really need me, I would try to be really good and maybe I would find a way to be needed there. I didn't know what else to do. I liked them so much that I was willing to realize that logically I was lucky to get asked to join the band at all, so I would have to be so helpful in everything, right? At least I could be a secretary or something, *anything*, because I wanted to be part of it.

"And they knew it. They understood I felt this way. And they were real careful and never made me feel unwanted. Christine very willingly gave me the stage, which I thought was very cool of a woman to say, 'Oh she's five years younger than me, and I've worked for 10 years on the road, killed myself, and here she is, our new frontwoman!' It was incredibly big of Christine to just move out of the way—because I do tend to kind of animate around. I drive Chris nuts. Crazy!" As a tribute to their friendship, Christine McVie wrote a song speculated to be about Stevie entitled "Friend." It was released in 2004 as the first track on her latest solo album, *In the Meantime.*

But it is "Rhiannon" that was and continues to be one of the songs that defines both Stevie Nicks and Fleetwood Mac. "'Rhiannon' is the heavy-duty song to sing every night, Stevie noted. "On stage it's really a mind tripper. Everybody, including me, is just blitzed by the end of it. And I put out so much in that song that I'm nearly down. There's something to that song that touches people. I don't know what it is but I'm really glad it happened."[6]

"Rhiannon," while proven to be a timeless lyric, also helped create the witch-mysticism that seems to surround Stevie. "I got the name from a novel, I think I bought it in an airport just before a long flight; it was called *Triad*, and it was about a girl named Rhiannon and her sister and mother, or something like that. I just thought the name was so pretty that I wanted to write something about a girl named Rhiannon. I wrote it about three months before I joined Fleetwood Mac, in about 1974. And then to find out that Rhiannon was a real mythical character! I went and read the four books of Rhiannon, and visited the lady who'd translated them. Rhiannon is the maker of birds, and the goddess of steeds; she's the protector of horses. Her music is like a pain pill. When you wake up and hear her birds singing her little song, the danger will have passed. I realized that somehow I had managed to pen a song that went very much along with the mythical tale of Rhiannon. That's when everybody started saying Stevie must be a black witch or something."[7]

Stevie has always perceived Rhiannon as a mystical figure who couldn't be tied down and in some ways felt uplifted throughout the song, like a seagull. As with all of Stevie's songs, this one is as autobiographical as the next. Stevie described her interpretation in an interview with *Music Connection.* "That song ['Rhiannon' (Will You Ever Win)] is really straight out of the old Welsh mythology. Rhiannon is the Goddess of Steeds and the Maker of Birds, and her song is a song that takes away pain. When you hear her song, you close your eyes and fall asleep, and when you wake up the pain is gone or the danger is gone and you'll see her three birds flying away. That's the legend. So, whenever I sing the song, I always think of that…" Sadly, Stevie was frequently in search of something to relieve her own pain.

Stevie's second contribution to the *Fleetwood Mac* album was her legendary "Landslide," a song that continues to be a timeless ballad. Stevie does her best writing during troubled times. "Landslide" was written when things weren't going well for her and Lindsey as a musical duo. On *VH1 Storytellers*, Stevie described how the song evolved: "The story of 'Landslide'…everybody seems to think that I wrote this song about them. Everybody in my family, all my friends, everybody…and my Dad, my Dad did have something to do with it, but he absolutely thinks that he was the whole complete reason it was ever written. I guess it was about September 1974, I was home at my Dad and Mom's house in Phoenix, and my father said, 'You know, I think that maybe…you really put a lot of time into this [her singing career], maybe you should give this six more months, and if you want to go back to school, we'll pay for it and uh, basically you can do whatever you want and we'll pay for it'—I have wonderful parents—and I went, 'Cool, I can do that.' [Then] Lindsey and I went up to Aspen…"

Before Stevie joined Fleetwood Mac, her family had a serious scare. Experiencing chest pain that couldn't be relieved by nitroglycerin, her father checked into the Mayo Clinic in Rochester, Minnesota. Jess Nicks was diagnosed with coronary artery disease and immediately underwent cardiac bypass surgery. Though he briefly returned to his high-stress corporate position, the chest pain came back and he retired at the age of forty-nine. Since Stevie wrote "Landslide" at approximately the same time, her father came to believe it was written for him. "The words are meant to portray the relationship between a parent and child," he told *Arizona Living*, almost in tears. "She wrote that song because she was fearful of my dying."

"'Landslide' I wrote in Aspen (in 1974). Three months before I joined Fleetwood Mac, along with 'Rhiannon.' And...that's where the snow-covered hills come from. And I was definitely doing a whole lot of reflecting when I was up there. He [Lindsey] came back to Aspen and he was very angry with me—and he left me—took Ginnie the poodle and the car and left me in Aspen the day that the Greyhound buses went on strike. I had a bus pass cuz my dad was president of Greyhound, I had a bus pass, I could go anywhere. I said, 'Fine, take the car and the dog, I have a bus pass.' I had a strep throat also. He drove away, I walk in and on the radio it says 'Greyhound Buses on strike all over the Unites States.' I'm going, oh no, I'm stuck. So in order to get out of Colorado I had to call my parents and they unwillingly sent me a plane ticket because they didn't understand what I was doing up there in the first place. So I follow him back to Los Angeles, that was like October, it was all around Halloween, two months later Fleetwood Mac called on New Years Eve."[8] She had just three months before her dad's six-month deadline for giving rock 'n' roll a go arrived.

In 2003, nearly thirty years later, Stevie received the nod for Song of the Year at the BMI Country Awards for "Landslide." A major hit for Stevie and Fleetwood Mac in 1975, it re-emerged as a single from the Dixie Chicks' *Home* album in 2003. The song was a hit across several genres including country, adult top 40 and adult contemporary. Even Smashing Pumpkins covered it, in 1994.

During the *Say You Will* tour in 2003, Stevie dedicated "Landslide" to Lindsey and said she wrote it for him and about him on the guitar he taught her to play. In January of 2004, she confided in *Q* magazine, "I wrote it—for him (Lindsey), about him. It's dear to both of us because it's about us. We're out there singing about our lives."

During an interview for *In the Studio with Red Beard*, Stevie described the feelings she had as she wrote the "Landslide" lyrics. "I realized then that everything could tumble, and when you're in Colorado, and you're surrounded by these incredible mountains, you think avalanche. It meant the whole world could tumble around us and the landslide would bring you down. And a landslide in the snow is like, deadly. And when you're in that kind of a snow-covered, surrounding place, you don't just go out and yell, because the whole mountain could come down on you.

"'Landslide' I wrote on the guitar, and it's another one that I wrote in about five minutes. But see, when I'm really thinking about something—I mean when something's really bothering me—again, the best thing that I can do is go to the music room, or to the office, where I can write. Because once I put it down and I can read it back, and I can think about what I'm saying, then it makes sense to me. When I'm just thinking it in my head, it's going around and around, and I feel like a little child unable to make a real, substantial decision. And we were talking about our lives...the rest of our lives." Just as "Landslide" has touched the hearts of many, songs touching Stevie's heart over the years include "Fire and Rain," by James Taylor, "Your Song," by Elton John, "Missing You," by John Waite, and "Hello It's Me," by Todd Rundgren.

"Crystal," Stevie's third contribution on the *Fleetwood Mac* album was a song from the *Buckingham Nicks* album. Although Stevie wrote the song, Lindsey sang it. She has said "Crystal" was written about her father and grandfather and that Lindsey does a better job with it than she does as the lead.

Soon after the completion of the tour promoting the *Fleetwood Mac* album, the band began working on *Rumours*, a collection of very intimate and personal songs resulting from the pain and strained relationships the two couples within the band experienced at the time. As work began on the album in the Record Plant in Sausalito, California, the band members were under extreme duress given the dissolution of both Stevie and Lindsey's relationship and the McVie's ensuing divorce. Yet they were able to put their personal problems aside. Their musical chemistry was just too good to throw away. Each one was way too proud and stubborn to walk away. Enjoying being in a band and making money, they had to grit their teeth and bear it.

With success came the realization that Stevie and Lindsey's relationship would never be quite the same. "We couldn't be together and also work together. I couldn't have him, you know, telling me that, you know, this song that I wrote wasn't that good and knowing he was saying that because he was angry about me because of our relationship. It just didn't leave us anywhere to go, anywhere to grow or get better."9

Lindsey too has come to realize the nature of the situation. "It's very difficult to be in the process of breaking up with someone and to have to see them everyday. It's just not natural, it's not healthy." During the making of *Rumours*, Stevie and I would have to work together. I mean I was the one who was sorting out her songs and making them into records. And there were times when I had the urge, not to want to do that, not to want to help her. It made for some hurtful times. It made for some times that were definitely rife with anger. And you had to push through anyway."

The way in which Stevie and Lindsey pushed through was by expressing their pain in songs such as "Dreams." Having lots of down time when her songs were not the area of focus and when she wasn't harmonizing vocals on Lindsey and Christine's work, Stevie took her portable Fender Rhodes piano to a studio adjacent to The Record Plant owned by Sly Stone. She told the story for *Classic Albums: Rumours*. "I think what happens with something like 'Dreams' the idea of writing it in Sly Stone's studio, black velvet bed with curtains you could pull...it just flowed out. It was written in about five minutes and I recorded it on a little cassette that way I wouldn't be nervous playing it for the band. Everybody really liked it and we recorded it right away."

"'Dreams' was about Lindsey and I—it was me trying to be philosophic once again. Whether or not I succeeded I don't know. I love the song 'Dreams.' I never get tired of singing 'Dreams.'"10

In the Studio with Fleetwood Mac captured Stevie's feelings when she wrote "Dreams" and described how she continues to capture those feelings over and over. "Love affairs are timeless, I mean, they don't change. That's why these songs [on *Rumours*] are timeless, I think. And that's why they're timeless to me and that's why I can walk out on the stage today and still sing them...and still feel the same way as when I wrote them is because I can remember so how I felt at that point, and I can remember the tears, and I can remember how hard it was for me to play 'Dreams' the first time, for the whole band, because I knew it would probably really upset Lindsey, and probably really upset Chris and John, and probably really upset Mick and really upset me. And if I could even get through it I'd be lucky."

While many consider Stevie and Lindsey's songs as melancholy and sometimes dark, Stevie does infuse positive themes. "I always put something at the end that says there's hope. You know, *When the rain washes you clean you'll know.* And that's an old Indian [Native American] custom…that if it rains—something like that—when somebody dies, if it rains their spirit is set free."[11]

Lindsey, unable to really appreciate Stevie's gift back then and in fact usually resenting how easily her songwriting came for her, has come to appreciate Stevie's hit song. "'Dreams' was an interesting outcome for something that didn't have a lot of variety in terms of its chord structures, but tons of variety in terms of its melodic left and right turns. There is no drama without contrast and we made the contrast out of all that…and it was a lot of fun."[12] Despite being sometimes resentful toward Stevie about engineering her music, he often enjoys working on her songs since she leaves them loose and allows him to work his magic.

While Stevie's solo albums are wonderful, no one can make her songs come alive like Lindsey Buckingham. In an interview with *Rolling Stone*, Lindsey shared his perspective on supporting Stevie's songs after things didn't work out for the couple romantically. "So you don't want to be my wife, my girlfriend, but you want me to do all that magic stuff on your songs. Is there anything else that you want, just, like, in my spare time?" He is truly the under-recognized and under-appreciated master of Fleetwood Mac. It has taken Mick many years to really understand Lindsey's contribution, and he is very grateful. Lindsey has described Mick as a totally different person since losing his cocaine habit. Despite personal and professional challenges over the years, they have become quite close.

The song that never made it to vinyl as one of the *Rumours* classics (until the re-mastered version was released) is "Silver Springs." During her BBC Radio interview, Stevie recalled how the song ended up as the B-side to "Go Your Own Way" instead of on the original *Rumours* album. "I wrote it for *Rumours*, and fourteen years ago I walked into the studio and the record was basically done. It was at the Record Plant, and Mick said,

'Stevie, I need you to come outside to the parking lot because I need to talk to you for a minute.' And I knew it was serious because Mick never asks you to go out to the parking lot for anything.

"So we walked to the huge Record Plant parking lot and he said, 'I'm taking "Silver Springs" off the record.' And, of course, my first reaction was, Why? And he said, 'There's a lot of reasons, but because basically it's just too long. And we think that there's another of your songs that's better, so that's what we want to do.' Before I started to get upset about 'Silver Springs,' I said, What other song? And he said, 'A song called "I Don't Want To Know."' And I said, But I don't want that song on this record. And he said, 'Well, then don't sing it.' And then I started to scream bloody murder and probably said every horribly mean thing that you could possibly say to another human being, and walked back in the studio completely flipped out.

"I said, 'Well, I'm not gonna sing "I Don't Want To Know." I am one-fifth of this band.' And they said. 'Well, if you don't like it, you can either (a) take a hike or (b) you better go out there and sing "I Don't Want To Know" or you're only gonna have two songs on the record.' And so, basically, with a gun to my head, I went out and sang 'I Don't Want To Know.' And they put 'Silver Springs' on the back of 'Go Your Own Way.'"

It was Stevie's mother who kept "Silver Springs" alive. In addition to owning the rights to the song, Stevie's mother, Barbara, named her Scottsdale antique shop The Silver Spring Emporium. With the release of the song as a single from *The Dance* album, "Silver Springs" is still very much alive even though it had to be retired during the *Say You Will* tour.

Ironically, "I Don't Want to Know" came from the Buckingham Nicks era. It was on the demo they brought with them to LA, and Stevie and Lindsey had performed it together many times. Twenty years later in 1997, Stevie was able to rationalize the situation. "I happen to really like that song...and I love singing that song [with Lindsey] because that was one of our Everly Brothers singing things that was really close and tight and really fun to sing...so if 'Silver Springs' was going to be replaced with anything, 'I Don't Want To Know' was a good replacement." Lindsey also shared his perspective. "We had to make a call on what the album needed. Kind of the group would edit in and out what was working and what wasn't. And that was great. At the eleventh hour to cut in something and have it be so straight ahead and it didn't require any pondering at all. That's the atypical song on *Rumours* for sure."[13]

Because "Silver Springs" was recorded for *The Dance*, their 1997 live reunion tour album and DVD, Stevie feels vindicated. She told the *Arizona Republic*, "In six weeks of rehearsal, it [performing 'Silver Springs' for the MTV special] was never like that. Only on Friday night did we let it go into something deeper. When we went on Friday, I knew we'd bring it out in case it was the last thing we'd ever do. The other shows were really, really good, but they weren't the show I wanted to leave behind. This show was...I wanted people to stand back and really watch and understand what [the relationship with Lindsey] was."[14] Lindsey's reaction was captured on *Classic Albums Fleetwood Mac Rumours*. "It's an interesting song in what it seems to be saying. Very bittersweet because she is talking about being my Silver Spring and what we could have been as lovers."

Stevie's final song on *Rumours* and the last track on the album is "Gold Dust Woman," a prolific tune that still receives tremendous airplay. While it is clearly a song about cocaine, Stevie explained in an interview with *Spin* that it was written before drugs hit the scene in a major way. "Well the gold dust refers to cocaine, but it's not completely about that, because there wasn't that much cocaine around then. Everybody was doing a little bit—you know, we never bought it or anything, it was just around—and I think I had a real serious flash of what this stuff could be, of what it could do to you. The whole thing about how we love the ritual of it, the little bottle, the diamond-studded spoons, the fabulous velvet bags. For me, it fit right into the candles and incense and all that stuff. And I really imagined that it could overtake everything, never thinking in a million years it would overtake me. I must have met a few people who I thought did too much coke, and I must have been impressed by that. Because I made it into a whole story."

On the imagery she continued, "The black widow, the dragon thing. It's all about being scared and angry." On the lyrics "rulers make bad lovers," she surmised, "I was definitely swept away about how big Fleetwood Mac was and how famous I suddenly was. Me, who couldn't buy anything before, could go in any store and buy anything I wanted. And I wondered what that would do to me on down the line. I might be a ruler, but maybe I'd be a lousy lover." Unfortunately, Stevie has remained without a steady love. She claims her busy schedule doesn't afford her an opportunity to have serious relationships.

On the *Classic Albums Fleetwood Mac Rumours* DVD, Stevie described the broader inspiration for the song. "'Gold Dust Woman' was a little bit about drugs. It was about, you know, keeping going. It was about cocaine. And you know after all these years since I haven't done any cocaine since 1986 I can talk about it now you know. But it was at that point...I don't think I had ever been so tired in my whole life as I was when we were like doing that. You know I think it was shocking me. The whole rock 'n' roll life was really heavy and it was so much work and it was so everyday intense you know. Being in Fleetwood Mac was like being in the army. It was like you have to be there. You have to be there and you have to be there as on time as you can be there. And even if there is nothing you have to do, you have to be there. So 'Gold Dust Woman' was really my kind of symbolic look at somebody going through a bad relationship, and doing a lot of drugs, and trying to just make it, trying to live, you know trying to get through it to the next thing."

To promote the release of *Rumours*, the band toured frenetically across the nation, often in station wagons. The *Rumours* tour lasted over a year and took Stevie and Lindsey to Europe and Australia for the first time. It was during that time Stevie and Mick began their initially clandestine romance. Stevie is quite open about her love affairs. She relayed the story of Don Henley, J.D. Souther, and Mick Fleetwood for *Spin*. "Well, when Lindsey and I broke up during *Rumours*, I started going out with Don Henley. And you know, I was like the biggest Eagles fan of life. And we went out, on and off, for about two years. He was really cute, and he was elegant. He is sexy. He's such an interesting guy.

"Here's one thing that Don did that freaked my band out so much. We're all in Miami, Fleetwood Mac and the Eagles. They're recording at this gorgeous house they'd rented on the water. It's totally romantic. It's pink. It's like Mar-a-Lago. Anyway, he sends a limousine driver over to our hotel with a box of presents for me, and they're delivered right into the breakfast room where everyone's eating. There's a stereo, a bunch of fabulous records. There's incredible flowers and fruits, beautiful. The limousine driver is taking all this out onto the table and I'm going, Oh, please, please, this is not going to go down well. And they want to know who it's from. And Lindsey is not happy. So I started going out with him. And this is not popular. Sure, Lindsey and I are totally broken up, I have every right in the world to go out with people, but…I spend most of my time with the band, and it's not real conducive to having a relationship.

"So, I went out with Don for awhile. I went out with [Eagles songwriter] J.D. Souther for awhile. We had an incredible time. And then I fell in love with Mick [Fleetwood]. And that went on for two years. Never in a million years could you have told me that would happen. That was the biggest surprise. Mick is definitely one of my great, great loves." On how things were between Lindsey and Mick, she continued, "That was not good. That was not good for anybody else in the band. Everybody was so angry, because Mick was married. To a wonderful girl and he had two wonderful children, and I was horrified. I loved these people. I loved his family. So it couldn't have possibly worked out. And it didn't. It just couldn't." Though their relationship didn't last very long, they did seem to find comfort in one another—apparently understanding what each other was going through at the time. "I was very much in love with Stevie," Mick explained for *VH1: Behind the Music.*

Mick Fleetwood described the evolution of their romantic relationship in his 1990 autobiography. "Our affair really began in Los Angeles even before we left for the Pacific. I'd sneak away from home to spend most of my time with Stevie, picking her up in one of my cars and driving along Mullholland. She was seeing a record executive, and I was married, and my parents were living with me, so everything was very secret, imbuing subsequent events with a kind of supercharged aura of romance. In Australia this blossomed into a full-on love affair.

"It started up in New Zealand. Late one night, after the concert, a Samoan limo driver took me and Stevie for a long cruise along the mountains and ridge backs at dawn. At one point we got out and walked a bit in silence, waiting for the sun to rise. There was a mist that turned to gentle rain, soaking us to our skin."

In an interview with *Independent Review*, Stevie described why their relationship didn't last. "That was a long, long time ago. It was like a little dream. What has lived, though, is that Mick and I still have a great love and respect for each other. Our relationship was so short that it didn't have time to build up animosities and jealousies. Mick will tell you—and I will tell you—that a lot of the reason it didn't continue was because we knew it would be the end of Fleetwood Mac. So we were very mature about that; we made the right decision. Mick and I were absolutely horrified that this happened. We didn't tell anybody until the very end, and then it blew up and was over. Lindsey and I have never, never talked about Mick. Ever."[15]

Despite his grief, Lindsey tried to demonstrate strength and acceptance of Stevie's relationship with Don Henley. "For Stevie, someone like Don Henley is good for her," he told *Crawdaddy* in 1976. "It's strange; it's one thing to accept not being with someone and it's another to see them with someone else, especially someone like Don, right? A big star in another group. I could see it coming and I really thought it was gonna bum me out, but it was really a good thing just to see her sitting with him. It actually made me happy. I thought there was something to fear but there wasn't. So the whole breakup has forced me to redefine my whole individuality—musically as well. I'm no longer thinking of Stevie and me as a duo. That thought used to freak me out but now it's made me come back stronger, to be Lindsey Buckingham."

The press often pegged Stevie as dating men that were only acquaintances. "I'm really starting to get angry. I mean I'm having all these relationships with all these guys that I don't know, that maybe I've met once, that I don't want to know and there's nothing I can do about it. All of a sudden I'm picking up these papers and I'm the Siren of the North. I'm really a very quiet lady and I love being at home."[16] She did admit dating another member of the Eagles lineup. "I went out with John David Souther for a while, who is very, very, very male chauvinistic and very sweet and cute and wonderful but very Texas, and I found when I was with him, I didn't mention Fleetwood Mac ever. It didn't help my status with the man to bring up anything I did, so I didn't. And then you start saying, 'But I work too. I'm happening. I write songs, but you aren't giving me a break.'"[17]

It was during the *Rumours* tour that Stevie began to have difficulties with her voice, as Peter Herbst's review of their Madison Square Garden concert on June 29, 1977 revealed. "Two things about Fleetwood Mac's Garden show: Stevie Nicks failing voice was the audience's prime discussion topic before and after the concert; and Fleetwood Mac performed magnificently without Nick's best efforts.

"Nicks clearly has become the group's centerpiece, a shaggy-haired love object who cultivates onstage mystique that only the very young could thoroughly buy. Her mannerisma—whirling dances (outstretched arms converting her shawl into butterfly wings), sotto voice introductions from Rhiannon: This is a song about a Welsh witch and sulky aimlessness between her numbers—skirt corniness. Still Nicks has an "undeniable" magnetism and gets away with her devices more often than not.

"On this night, though, she couldn't summon the chops to get away with anything, Fleetwood Mac had canceled their previous evening's performance in Syracuse because Nicks was suffering from severe vocal strain. At the Garden she found it impossible to hit "Rhiannons" higher notes—though she struggled valiantly. And during "Gold Dust Woman", Nicks, wearing a witch's black hat and framed by a Halloween moon that reappeared from time to time during the night growled hoarse incarnations to rival Linda Blair's Regan's without Regan's exquisite control.

"Even more, Nicks was nearly always physically unstable. She lurched about the stage, twirled slowly with all the grace of a drunken sailor and, near the concert's end, wobbled along the stage's pit and starboard precipices while frantic roadies followed to prevent a fall."

Even though Stevie enjoyed the riches of fame, she dealt with her demanding schedule, her breakup with Lindsey, and her short-lived relationship with Mick by turning to cocaine. "In the first couple of years it was very, very much something to get energy from, you know. Oh I'll never get through this if I don't do some coke, you know. I've got fifteen interviews, I've got a show, I've got twenty fittings, I've got this, that. I can't do it all, I'm too tired. So yeah it was like, you know, it was like, like taking one of your mom's diet pills."[18]

"There was cocaine, and there was champagne—a lot of it. It just dropped into everybody's lap at the same time, and everybody I knew—people who had no money, people who had money—everybody did coke. It was a pretty unfortunate universal thing."[19] Being in a major rock 'n' roll band placed Stevie in an atmosphere she has described as one big outrageous morning-till-night party everyday, for many years.

"In the beginning, [stimulants] made you brave," she told Jenny Boyd for her *Musicians in Tune* publication. "You're scared to walk onstage in front of a bunch of people. Last night in front of only two hundred people, my knees were knocking together. I was holding onto the microphone and my hand was shaking because I was so nervous. The old days to get away from that you have a drink, or whatever anybody else does, and you get brave and so you don't have to experience that terrible fear. I get terrible stage fright...where I'm very, very nervous. [But] the second I am onstage I'm not nervous anymore...[Stage fright] is probably why in the old days people did start doing drugs and stuff because they were simply afraid. Then that becomes a habit, then you think you absolutely can't do without it."

The success achieved from the *Rumours* album created a climate of extreme excesses. The band went out and bought houses and cars. Their hard work paid off in more ways than just financially. In 1978, Fleetwood Mac's *Rumours* was honored with the Grammy Award for Album of the Year, having competed with Steely Dan's *Aja*, James Taylor's *J.T.*, The Eagles's *Hotel California*, and *Star Wars: John Williams conducting the London Symphony Orchestra*. On January 24, 2003, *Rumours* was inducted into the Grammy Hall of Fame and continues to be one of the best selling albums of all time.

Rumours has been re-mastered in DVD Dolby Digital 5.1 format and was released along with the re-mastered versions of *Fleetwood Mac* and *Tusk* on March 23, 2004. "Silver Springs" has now been added to the song line up, where, as Stevie would tell you, it should have been all along. Years have gone by and lots of healing has occurred. Mick put it well when he said, "Now I can rest easy. I was the unfortunate person who had to tell Stevie it wasn't going on the album. Well now you can forgive me, Stevie."[20]

Following the *Rumours* tour, Fleetwood Mac returned to the studio to capture their musical synergy once more. But the phenomenal success of their previous album placed tremendous pressure on the band. Their next album needed to be just as good; people expected a *Rumours* II sound. Lindsey and Mick, however, wanted to do something completely different.

Influenced by the new wave bands, Lindsey's preference was to portray less pop and go for a new and fresher sound that allowed him to demonstrate the breadth of his guitar competencies. Given his mastery and persuasive nature, the band acquiesced. *Tusk* ultimately performed admirably according to many standards, yet it sold considerably fewer copies than its predecessor, and Lindsey took the blame. Though "Sara" and "Tusk" were top ten hits, critics generally felt the album was a collection of solo contributions rather than a cohesive collaboration. If fans knew then that "tusk" was Mick's pet term for his "male member," as he called it in his autobiography, who knows what it could have done! When Stevie discovered the name of the album was going to be *Tusk*, she threatened to leave the band in revulsion. Mick chose to ignore her and nothing ever came of it.

Over the years, *Tusk* has earned the respect of many diehard fans. Stevie, on the other hand, was not very happy with the album at the time. "Well, *Tusk* wasn't *my* album. *Tusk* was mainly Lindsey's conception, dream, everything he ever wanted to do. Everybody just figured that for whatever his reasons were, it was important that he do that and we just sort of sat back and let him do it. I don't mean to sound blasé or anything. I was there. I just didn't have very much to do with it. Because if I had had much to do with it, it wouldn't have been a double album and it wouldn't...it wouldn't have been crazy."[21] Stevie has also described the studio created for the making of *Tusk* as an African tribal ground or movie set. Mick had lived in Africa for seven years as a child. She looks back on the experience as one of the nicest because it was the weirdest. They had so much stuff in the studio, it took a week and a semi truck to move it all out.

After all these years, Stevie has learned to appreciate *Tusk*. It took the band thirteen months to record the album, and as she told *BAM* magazine, "When you listen to all those songs for 13 months, it's a drain…So for me, it was way ahead of its time. I was there and I sang on it, but I didn't have a real connection with it. And now I really, really like it. I have these incredible speakers, I like to just lie on the floor and listen to it. It sounds so cool."

Stevie contributed five songs to the double album, with "Sara" creating the most speculation and fervor. Fans still spend an inordinate amount of time deciphering her lyrics and searching the media coverage to determine their personal interpretation of the real story. While Stevie is typically very forthcoming about the inspiration for her lyrics, she has been vague about the meaning of "Sara," one of her favorite and most personal songs.

The speculation started when Don Henley's interview with *Gentlemen's Quarterly* in 1991 described his "prodigious romantic escapades" and highlighted his affair with Stevie Nicks. Henley was quoted as saying, "I believe to the best of my knowledge [Stevie Nicks] became pregnant by me. And she named the [unborn] kid Sara, and she had an abortion and then wrote the song of the same name to the spirit of the aborted baby. I was building my house at the time, and there's a line in the song that says 'And when you build your house, call me.'"

On whether the line indeed references Don Henley—whom she was dating at the time—Stevie told *Us* magazine: "That is true. He did [build the house]. And I was in it before he finished it." She went on to say that "'Sara' [is my most personal song]. It's about myself, and what all of us in Fleetwood Mac were going through at the time. The true version of that song is sixteen minutes long. It's a saga with many verses people haven't heard." While Stevie admitted that "'Sara' was pretty much about Mick," for *MTV Fanatic,* she clarified further. "So, he was the 'great dark wing.' And, ah, it was about everything that was going on at that particular time, too, but he was the, the reason for the, you know, the beginning of it." The honest person that she is, Stevie left the door open for other interpretations by saying that only the beginning was written for Mick.

In an article written for the *Parade* Sunday newspaper magazine, Stevie was asked about Don Henley's claim that she aborted his baby and wrote the song about the episode. The magazine reported, "Stevie Nicks, 43, won't comment on Henley's revelation, replying that they 'remain friends.'" Stevie was also asked about Henley's *GQ* comment in an interview with Mary Turner. She responded by saying, "Don had to make many an apologetic phone call."

Understandably, it's a very personal subject. Losing a child does seem to fit with the "Sara" lyrics: "Now it's gone, it doesn't matter what for," and "There's a heartbeat and it never really died." "Goodbye Baby"—the eighteenth track on the *Say You Will* album, which was also known as "The Tower"—a song written much earlier with several minor lyrical alterations, has circulated among fans for years and could also be interpreted as referring to the loss of a child.

Another clear theme is predicated on her sudden loss of love and companionship. In October of 1978, Mick fell for and ultimately married Sara Recor, one of Stevie's best friends. It was hard on Stevie losing another love, and, as always, she dealt with the pain through her songs. For months after losing Mick to Sara, Stevie told *Mojo*, "We weren't talking to each other very much. We were there, but looking past each other. Everybody was nervous: 'Is she going to burst into tears and leave?'"

Upon the release of "Sara," in 1980, a lawsuit was filed by Carol L. Hinton of Rockford Michigan claiming she'd submitted the lyrics to Warner Brothers in November 1978. Stevie submitted a demo copy from July 1978 to the Court. To avoid a long court battle, Stevie's attorneys settled out of court for $1,500. "There were some great similarities [in the lyrics], and I never said she didn't write the words she wrote," she told *Rolling Stone*. "Just don't tell me I didn't write the words I wrote. Most people think that the other party will settle out of court, but she picked the wrong songwriter. To call me a thief about my first love, my songs, that's going too far."

"Sara" is considered Stevie's most complicated and ambiguously written song. Stevie went for years without singing it onstage due to the personal pain it evoked. "If I ever have a little girl," she told Jim Ladd, "I will name her Sara. It's a very special name to me. I love singing it on stage. It's the absolute delight of my night. There's so much in 'Sara.' And it is—the poet in my heart, for sure."

During the *Say You Will* tour, Stevie sang it beautifully. She told her audience that she thought she would never sing it in a live setting and that it is very special to her. The lyrics for the original sixteen-minute version of "Sara" have not been released and have never been sung onstage. It is likely that they would provide a clearer understanding of the inspiration for the song while painting a picture of Stevie's emotional state and circumstances at the time.

Clearly, whatever the connection with the name Sara, it is a strong one. When Stevie checked herself into Betty Ford for her cocaine addiction in 1986, she assumed the name Sara Anderson. In fact, "Welcome to the Room…Sara," from the *Tango in the Night* album is Stevie's description of her experience at Betty Ford. Throughout the years of fame and success, Stevie has often been asked about her plans for having a family. Her responses have been ambivalent at best. It seems that Sara is Stevie's alter ego or muse. It is impossible to know whether Sara is the musical starlet or the one who would like to get married and have a baby.

Stevie's second contribution on the *Tusk* album was "Storms." In an interview with Jim Ladd in 2005, she provided insight into the song that, until then, had been purely speculation. "Always been a Storm [Storms] was written about my relationship with Mick and,…it was written when it [the relationship] was over and when I was very very upset about it and,…like we said, great tragedy can turn around and make you say things that you may never say otherwise. 'Every night that goes between, I feel a little less, as you slowly walk away from me, this is only another test,' that's talking about…wisdom. In the wisdom of understanding that this relationship was not going to be anymore came that beautiful poem. And, that's probably one of the songs that I'm most proud of, and of course, that was probably one of the most terrible times of my life was getting over the idea that Mick and I weren't going to be together."

"Living through each empty night, a deadly call inside" may relate to the physical and emotional needs that were met by their relationship. "I did not deal with the road" is reference to touring while coping with pain and loss. "I've always been a storm" speaks to Stevie's inability to deal with situations in a healthy and calm manner, as does "I've never ever been a blue calm sea." With "So I try to say goodbye, my friend," she seems to say the relationship was temporary but the memories were long-lived. Similarly, "I should have known from the start, I'd be the broken hearted" is a common theme in Stevie's songs. She described herself as being a "fool once more" in "Beautiful Child."

"Sisters of the Moon" is Stevie's third song from the *Tusk* album, and, according to Mick Fleetwood's autobiography, was written during one of the early Fleetwood Mac tours. The song is reflective of her loneliness while on tour and the difficulties of becoming famous. She starts the song with "intense silence as she walked in the room." She considered the room her rock 'n' roll lifestyle. There was always a crowd around, but she heard an intense silence. "Does anybody know her name" speaks to how fame put her in the spotlight but few really knew her. The "cruel people" are those who kept expecting more and more from her. Stevie was in need of the friends she knew before she became famous. She pushed herself so hard and felt compelled to use cocaine just to meet the expectations of fame. Her ambivalence toward fame is also mentioned in "I Miss You," a song from 2001's *Trouble in Shangri-La,* her seventh solo album. She refers to Lindsey and describes him as the one who can best convey love, pain, strained relationships, and fame to her. Yet, at the end of the day, she has said Fleetwood Mac was the best thing in her life and a dream come true, despite all the nightmares.

"Angel," Stevie's fourth song on the album, was also written for Lindsey Buckingham. It's consistent in keeping with one of her common themes, how "true-great love" had passed her by. "Sweet Girl," Stevie's new song for *The Dance* album, had a similar yet more historical message. She wrote, "Everyone said I'd never love" and described how she has not had many long-term relationships since she chose to "dance across the stages of the world." When *Tusk* was released in 1979, Stevie and Lindsey were no longer together as a couple. They were, however, ensconced in each other's daily lives. She wrote, "Sometimes the most beautiful things, the most innocent things" and "many of those dreams keep passing us by." These lyrics demonstrate her regret that their relationship—and other relationships—had ended.

In many ways, Lindsey contributed greatly to Stevie's success, or at least helped put her in a position to succeed. As such, it is not difficult to see why she would refer to him as her angel. Lindsey too has used this metaphor in songs written about Stevie. For example, Lindsey's "Goodbye Angel" from the *Mirage* outtakes was written a few years after Stevie's "Angel," saying good-bye to her just as he did in "Say Goodbye" on the *Say You Will* album.

During the *Tusk* documentary when Lindsey and Stevie were practicing "Angel," she sang, "You feel good, it's funny that you understood, when you were good, you were very good." At this point in the song, their eyes locked and they smiled. Stevie spoke of this "Angel" moment in the *Tusk* documentary. "There's this thing that goes on between us. It always has and probably always will. It was scary watching that because you could see everything that went down between them in the last 10 years."

Stevie revealed a lot about herself in the song. Her theme of ambivalence is clear once more as she swings from confused, desperate, and unsure girl to independent woman within the same song. She remembers the submissive girl in comparison to her stronger, free, and self-reliant persona. In the *Tusk* interview with Jim Ladd, he asked Stevie to interpret "so I close my eyes softly 'til I become that part of the wind" and to define a "charmed hour." In her reply, she referred to the story of Rhiannon "becoming the part of the wind...a peaceful sleep that is void of any pain." She defined the charmed hour as "the best hour of your life."

"Beautiful Child," Stevie's fifth song on *Tusk,* is a remarkable ballad and one that she was finally able to sing live during the *Say You Will* tour in 2003 and 2004. This beautiful yet sad song was written about Stevie's affair with Mick Fleetwood, given their age difference and the secretive and taboo nature of their relationship. It was the love that could never be.

A theme of contradiction runs throughout this autobiographical lyric as well. She wants to leave, but he won't send her away and she doesn't have the strength to leave on her own. She knows the relationship is wrong but doesn't want to give it up. She is not a child yet is still naïve and trusting. She is dependent but tries to exert her independence. She loves him but knows she can't have him. Again, Stevie "seeks the mother she knew" by putting herself in painful and chaotic relationships and situations. The idea that women must be cared for and should strive to marry and have children rather than pursue a demanding career continues to be a common thread in our society. This conflict is evident in Stevie's music and often a topic in her many interviews.

In an interview with *People* magazine, Stevie was as transparent as ever when asked about love. "[Male rockers are] pretty chauvinistic. I strive to be taken seriously as a writer, and be as good as they are. So they resent my success. I see it in their eyes: 'How did this dingbat manage to get everything she wants?'" She went on to explain how the Fleetwood Mac work ethic got in the way. "How many men, even the nicest, most patient can understand that for months you will come home at 7 A.M., dead tired and in a bad mood? For now the band is all there is room for in my life. It's just as well. On the road, no man can get within 10 feet. I hardly ever meet any new men."

The lifestyle was getting to Stevie by 1979 and she was forced to make some financial decisions. Fearing she wouldn't make the kind of money to which she'd become accustomed since the release of *Rumours* and not wanting to "come out of this absolutely helpless," she sold her large Tudor home above Sunset Boulevard, commonly referred to as Fantasyland by the men she dated. Instead, she chose a modest beachfront condominium. It was only recently that Stevie purchased a larger home two blocks away. She plans to keep the same ambiance in her new place but needed more room for entertaining family and friends. "Some people thrive on being a rock star," she told *People* magazine. "I hate it. I don't like being waited on all the time, people following me around saying, 'Let me do this, let me do that.'"

Despite Stevie's reservations about the lifestyle, the *Tusk* tour was one of Fleetwood Mac's most extreme rock star excesses. The tour was scheduled to go on for a year, and the band decided they were going to be comfortable. With a chartered airline, limousines for everyone (including their stage crew), luxurious hotel suites painted pink for the girls, and all the cocaine you can imagine, they survived.

The most successful band of the seventies, Fleetwood Mac was poised for ongoing fame and fortune. The eighties would bring two albums, but also heartbreak and strife when Lindsey decided to leave the band after *Tango in the Night*. The eighties also revealed Stevie's unprecedented ability to balance her place in a major rock 'n' roll band with the launch of an incredibly successful solo career.

Fleetwood Mac—mid '70s
(Photo by Thom Westhof)

Stevie—mid '70s
(Photo by Neil Zlozower)

Stevie in Los Angeles, 1976
(© Roger Ressmeyer / CORBIS)

Fleetwood Mac—1977
(© Bettman / CORBIS)

Fleetwood Mac—1978
(Chris Walter / Photofeatures)

Stevie with her mom, Barbara Nicks—The 20th
Annual Grammy Awards, Shrine Auditorium,
Los Angeles, CA, February 23, 1978
(Ron Galella / WireImage)

Stevie—Brussels' Forest National on June 12, 1980
(© *Philippe Carly—www.newwavephotos.com*)

Four

Stevie's Solo Career Soars with *Bella Donna* and *The Wild Heart*

In 1977, Stevie met Paul Fishkin, a record executive who was sure Stevie could make it on her own. "She was the hottest female singer in the world, at the time, albeit in a group, not as a solo artist."[1] Being the mad songwriter, she also had all kinds of songs that would never get recorded by Fleetwood Mac. Paul believed in her then and has been there for her through the good and the bad times. He never doubted she could sell millions of records.

Together they created Modern Records, Inc. in 1980 with Danny Goldberg and began transforming Stevie from band member to solo act. "Paul Fishkin and I believed in her," stressed Goldberg. "We both risked our careers on her, but we all had a dream. Stevie's the real thing. She gets her motivation from the heart."[2] By 2000, with seven solo releases on the Modern Records label, she had sold over 15 million albums. Stevie remained a major shareholder in the company until 1996 when she bought out her contract and the agreement to the box set release. She is now under contract with Reprise, a subsidiary of Warner Brothers.

Stevie remembered the evolution of the record company and her solo career for *Rock* magazine. "I decided to do *Bella Donna* when I came off the road with Fleetwood Mac at the end of the *Tusk* tour. I was really in terrible shape. I was so tired and sung out. I was so 'Landslide-ed' out and so 'Rhiannon-ed' out that I thought if I had to stand on stage for two and one-half hours and do that set one more time I was going to go nuts. The idea to do a solo album came when I was going out with Paul Fishkin about four years ago [1979]. We just sat down one night and decided that it would be wonderful to start a record company that really cared about the artists and had high morals and principles and was special. And he did it. He moved the Ferris wheel and started Modern. It was very difficult for both of us. Everybody was angry at us. But we really felt that it was important that we go ahead and do it no matter what."

Stevie found solace in her relationship with Paul Fishkin. She needed someone in her life that would just be there for her, without question. As she often does, Stevie isolated her rock 'n' roll lifestyle as the reason she rarely had a steady relationship. "It's not easy to be involved with a lady singer who's always gone," she told *People*. "Paul is sweet and wonderful and understands as well as anyone. I'm not interested in playing around, but I do get terribly lonely on the road." Stevie's loneliness has come out in her songs over the years. Now as she travels with Fleetwood Mac and is often in the company of the families of John McVie, Mick Fleetwood, and Lindsey Buckingham, she must still be lonely. Luckily, Stevie's brother and father have often joined her for the West Coast concerts.

One can only imagine the stress on Stevie and her Fleetwood Mac mates when she finally told them about the plans for her solo career. She was determined to do both, and that worried them from two perspectives. They were concerned it could hurt Fleetwood Mac, regardless of whether it was highly successful or flopped. But Stevie was sure her solo career would not hurt her band. She wasn't going to let it.

"My relationship with Fleetwood Mac will never change. I will always be the baby sister, the one that is left out a little bit. My solo work allows me not to feel bad about it and enjoy them for what they are, instead of worrying about not being included enough. That's what I used to get upset about. They were not even close to using my full potential. But now I know I have something else to go to."[3]

When Ray Rodgers at *Interview* magazine queried the level of support she received from Fleetwood Mac for her solo career, she had this to say. "Supportive is a pretty big word. They were not supportive. When I first went to do *Bella Donna*, they questioned my reasons, and once they realized that I was simply looking for an outlet for my songs—because three songs for Fleetwood Mac every two years just wasn't enough—they understood I wasn't trying to leave the band. Then it just became something else I did." It was a relief to Stevie to be free of the Fleetwood Mac studio, where she often had little to do as the others worked endless hours arranging their songs.

Fishkin felt it was important that Stevie be branded a pure rock 'n' roll singer rather than a Fleetwood Mac-inspired ethereal entity. "She was a rocker, you know, her whole thing was Janis Joplin, so we really worked hard, very consciously to go after, make sure we had a rock song or two as the first single. We knew that we had to lock in the rock guys, you know, the rock programmers and the rock stations and we also knew that a lot of those guys even though they kind of like the way she looked, but didn't quite take her seriously because of that sort of witch, airy fairy image that kind of came out of the Fleetwood Mac thing."[4]

The plan worked. Moreover, Stevie was finally given an opportunity to infuse her country influence and release songs that Fleetwood Mac would never have recorded. It's quite a range, going from "After the Glitter Fades" to "Edge of Seventeen" on the same album, a testament to Stevie's gift as a songwriter and phenomenal talent as a singer. Stevie let *Rock* magazine know that it was just easier to let Fleetwood Mac do what they wanted to do with her songs. "When I give a song to Fleetwood Mac they kind of take it apart and put it back together. So if it was country, it's not country anymore. You wouldn't ever hear the country in it. I don't mind it but if I really don't like it I tell them. I let a lot of songs be done in a way that I really wouldn't do them but, because it makes everybody else happy, I go along. I figure it's not going to make my song any better to have them play it the way I want it and have them play it terribly."

Jimmy Iovine was chosen to produce Stevie's first album and eventually became her romantic interest as well. Stevie's pattern of dating strong men in the business continued. He was concerned that Stevie was accustomed to the studio excesses from Fleetwood Mac, so he immediately mandated strict boundaries. Iovine shot straight with her. He told her that making a record is not a part-time job. He wanted to approach it as if she'd never made an album before. The seasoned studio musicians brought on board needed to see this as more than just one of her hobbies. If it was just a hobby, Iovine wasn't interested.

"Record producer Jimmy [Iovine] expected a lot from me from the very beginning. Well, he did bring me back to some reality. My life had to change in order to do an LP with him. I had to change. I couldn't be Stevie Nicks with Fleetwood Mac. I had to be much stronger and much more in control of myself, because he would not waste his time working with an out-of-control, flaky girl singer with Fleetwood Mac. He had no reason to be in the studio with that person and it was made very clear to me from the very beginning that if I was gonna do this, I was no longer the coddled, dependent baby of Fleetwood Mac.

"He said, 'This is not big rock 'n' roll. This is something you have never done before, you are not a proven solo artist in any way, shape, or form. You have been protected like the little baby egg for seven years. This is something that you have to do alone, Stevie, and if you want to do this then I have to know that you are going to be very, very strong and very disciplined.'"[5]

Stevie's preferred style of recording was the polar opposite of Fleetwood Mac, so it was not difficult for her to live up to Jimmy's expectations—most of the time. Rather than technically belabor every note, she wanted to go in, play the demo for the band, let them react, and then record it. She focused on how it would sound to someone sitting at home or driving in a car. She went for more of a rock concert sound. When she tried to interject too much of her style, Jimmy would remind her that he was running the show. Oddly enough, she accepted it. Perhaps he was more pleasant about it than Lindsey had purportedly been.

In July of 1981, Stevie released *Bella Donna*, her first solo album. It was an instant success. It hit the Billboard chart as the number one album and remained there for a week. Within two months, record sales approached the two million mark. Consequently, Stevie was crowned the "Queen of Rock and Roll" by *Rolling Stone* on September 3, 1981.

The album was eventually certified as quadruple platinum. "I don't have a great voice," Stevie confided. "But, I do have a voice that makes people stop and listen. I did the album because I wanted to make sure that I could still do something for myself. I was really kind of stunned [about the record's rapid chart ascension]. I never let myself believe that the best thing is going to happen."[6]

"I dreamed only about giving a little fairy tale to people," she told *High Times*. "That's what the outfit is on my album cover, that's what that bird is. That bird belongs to my brother, that's the only reason I could work with a wild animal. That's Max on the front. The outfit I wear on the cover of *Bella Donna* is the same as the one I wore on *Rumours*, except it's opposite, it's white. It's a strange turn-around that I've come from black to white." To get the right sound for her songs, Stevie would help her band members understand the meaning of her often-obtuse lyrics. "To explain to [guitarist/vocalist] Waddy [Wachtel] that "Bella Donna" was serious—I was not talking about a beautiful woman. I was talking about a beautiful woman becoming old and not beautiful. And skinny and too tired, the woman disappears."

Stevie has said *Bella Donna* alludes to the way in which she recaptured a little bit of her life. She was starting to doubt herself after seven years with Fleetwood Mac. Her life was completely, undeniably wrapped around the band. "I just decided when I came off that tour [*Tusk*] that I was not going to give up my life and die a lonely, overdone, overused rock star.

"There's no glamour in that. I don't want to be written up in 50 years as a miserable old woman who never got to do anything but tour and be famous for ten years and then it was over. I'm far too intelligent to not know that there will be a time when I won't be 33 anymore, when I won't be that pretty anymore, and I'll be tired. I want to know that I can still have fun and function on my own and be part of the world. That's why I made this album alone. I can't give my life away anymore for Fleetwood Mac. That was an important realization for me."[7]

"Bella Donna," the title song on the album, related what was going on in Stevie's life at the time. It's a cautionary tale on the prizes and pitfalls of superstardom. Having come off the road from an exhausting tour with Fleetwood Mac, she needed to sort out her life. *Bella Donna* was about me, wondering if I could take anymore of the rock 'n' roll lifestyle," she told David Criblez of *The Island Ear*. "It was about deciding how I could keep my music and still stay in touch with reality. There were times mentally when I would think, I don't think I can do this anymore." "Bella Donna" meant beautiful lady and poisonous herb, and Stevie felt trapped somewhere between the two images.

"Kind of Woman" was also very personal. "Well, this has to be Lindsey's song. 'Cause I wrote this song about Lindsey…in 1973, we weren't exactly rolling in the money. And Lindsey got an offer to go on the road with the Everly Brothers, minus one brother. But Lindsey and me were the original, after-the-Everly-Brothers-Everly Brothers! And…we needed money, and he didn't want to work as a waitress, so he went. And I was…jealous and very heartsick and very bummed out that I didn't get to go. In fact, I was really, really unhappy about it. So I wrote this song about what I thought it would be for somebody who was, you know, I mean, Lindsey was *darling*, and I thought, 'Somebody's gonna snag him out there for sure!' And so I was imagining the groupies with the black feathers and the rhinestones and the boots and the black stockings, and I was dying. I was like, 'So right, I get to go to work every morning, and *you* are out there on the road being an Everly Brother!' So 'Kind of Woman' was, you know, 'You didn't mean to meet her.' Right, right, you're gonna call me and tell me that?"[8]

"Think About It" was written for Christine McVie. Though she and Stevie were in relationships that were falling apart, they both realized they had so much to lose if they were to walk away from the successes of Fleetwood Mac. Stevie wanted to be strong for her friend when she was sad.

"After the Glitter Fades" was actually written in 1972 before Stevie's stardom began. The *Buckingham Nicks* album had just been dropped by the record company, and her house was filled with musicians Waddy Wachtel, Warren Zevon, and others recording demos with Lindsey. She clearly had a premonition of what would later occur in her life. She initially wanted Dolly Parton to sing the song but wasn't successful in getting the music into Dolly's hands for her consideration.

Stevie wrote "Outside The Rain" as the one link on the album between herself and Fleetwood Mac. She felt that it could have been a Fleetwood Mac song given the chord similarities with "Dreams" and "Sara" and because the band was still very much a part of her life. Stevie has often said "How Still My Love" is one of her favorites on the *Bella Donna* album. The lyrics reflect, once again, her feelings about sacrificing love for fame.

Stevie loved singing duets and as a component of her solo career joined forces with famous artists such as Don Henley, Tom Petty, and Kenny Loggins. She had an ability to mold her unique voice, yet her harmony was immediately recognizable and unforgettable. Tom Petty's "Stop Draggin' My Heart Around," a duet they sang together for the *Bella Donna* album, was nominated for Best Vocal Performance by a Duo or Group after hitting the pop charts at number three. A year later, the National Association of Recording Merchandisers declared *Bella Donna* the best-selling album by a female artist for the second consecutive year. It is the only time an album has achieved that status two years in a row.

Tom Petty has said that with Stevie, "It's like when you've got a sister in the family nobody wants to talk about much. You know what I mean? Sure, someone you love but who's a little bit, er, different."[9] Ultimately, Stevie and Tom Petty developed a very close friendship. She spent many a night at his house while he played the guitar and they sang. "He'll say I'm like a plane that doesn't have any radar," she told *Raw*. "He says to me, 'You're not living in the real world,' and I'm saying, 'Do you live in the real world Tom?' And he's going, Well *I* live in more of a real world than *you* do for sure."

When asked about her duet with Kenny Loggins, Stevie had this to say. "That was a discipline thing. I call him Slave-Driver Loggins. He cracked the whip on me for two days to get that particular performance. And I was downright angry at points where I was going, 'I'm not going to do this.' He said, 'Yes, you are.' He's a real good producer, Kenny; he got exactly what he wanted. When it was done and I left, I was knocked out. I really had to keep my mouth shut and do what I was told. And it worked. He wasn't interested in a dull vocal."[10] The outcome, "Whenever You Call Me a Friend," is an amazing song that highlights the beauty of her harmonization with a very talented male vocalist.

"I just love singing with people and they know it," she told *Rock* magazine. "So when people call me up they know I'll come down 'cause I just love to sing duets. That's how the duets come about. "Leather and Lace" I wrote for Waylon Jennings and Jessi Colter who were going to do an album five years ago. Waylon had asked me to write a song called "Leather and Lace" and I spent a long time on it. I tried to give it a little bit of Waylon, a little bit of Jessi and a little bit of what I knew it was like to be in show business, what it was like to work with your husband or your old man. But they (Jennings and Colter) broke up, and Waylon decided he was going to do it alone."

"But I said no, because I had put a lot of time into the psychology of the song and felt it was a mistake to do it alone. It's a wonderful song. So when *Bella Donna* came out, there was no reason for it not to be done just because Waylon and Jessi broke up. But I did want everyone to know I wrote the song for them. I didn't write it for myself." Stevie was dating Don Henley at the time. She would play it for him periodically, and he would tell her it was terrible and advise her to start over. When he finally determined the song was acceptable, they recorded a demo together that was quite similar to the final version released on *Bella Donna*.

Stevie wrote "Highwayman" about what a woman in rock 'n' roll has to do to keep up with the men. "I wrote it about Don Henley," she told Jim Ladd. "And I actually, in fact, wrote it because I considered him, and all of his crazy gang, to be the highwaymen. There's an old English poem, it's not English, it's just an old, old poem about the highwayman comes riding, riding, and he's coming riding down, the pale rider against the moon, and they've got Bess the innkeeper's daughter, and she's tied up in the barn, and when he comes through the door, her hand's gonna move and flip the trigger and it's gonna kill him. So it's an amazing poem, that, somewhere in school, you might remember it. So somewhere between, you know, Don Henley and the Eagles and that, I thought that these were the highwaymen, that these were, in my world, they *were* the highwaymen. So that's what I wrote it about. And I was going out with Don for quite awhile, actually, so that was really the song that I actually wrote about Don. That's why he's singing and playing on it."

By February of 1982, "Edge of Seventeen," the third single from the album, had entered the charts and climbed to number eleven. It was nominated for Best Rock Vocal Performance by a Female Artist at the 24th Annual Grammy Awards. The immediate inspiration came from Jane Petty, Tom's wife. She met Tom at the age of seventeen and when telling Stevie the story with her Southern accent, it sounded like *edge* of seventeen. Stevie described the meaning of the song further.

"'Edge of Seventeen' closes it [the album]—chronologically, anyway—with the loss of John Lennon and an uncle at the same time. That song is sort of about how no amount of money or power could save them. I was angry, helpless, hurt, and sad."[11] Stevie gave more specifics while speaking with *Rolling Stone*. "The line 'And the days go by like a strand in the wind' that's how fast those days were going by during my uncle's illness, and it was so upsetting to me. The part that says, 'I went today…maybe I will go again…tomorrow' refers to seeing him the day before he died. He was home and my aunt had some music softly playing, and it was a perfect place for the spirit to go away. The white-winged dove in the song is a spirit that is leaving a body, and I felt a great loss at how both Johns were taken. 'I hear the call of the nightbird singing…come away…come away…'"

Not everyone afforded Stevie accolades for her album. David Gans with *The Record* had this to say, "Between her songs and the way she appears to be conducting her life, Stevie Nicks comes off as a modern-day equivalent to the movie queens of the '30s, reaching inside herself for some ill-defined personal misery to fuel her creative machinery."

No one really knows Stevie any better than Lindsey Buckingham. He was perplexed that even her success with *Bella Donna* didn't give her what she was looking for. "In all the time I have known her, Stevie has never been very happy, and I don't think the success of her album has made her any happier. In fact it may have made her less happy."[12]

Stevie was never really able to celebrate *Bella Donna's* success. She took a personalized copy of her album to Lindsey, placing it in the area of the studio where he often worked. Yet Stevie says he never took it home. And it certainly wasn't something she could celebrate with the collective Fleetwood Mac. She wanted to keep it out of their face so it wouldn't hurt them. They didn't even talk about it.

It was Stevie who was hurting. On the very day her album reached number one, she received devastating news. "When *Bella Donna* came out," she told *BAM* magazine, "Fleetwood Mac was at the top of their game. It was the most incredible time. But then my best friend, Robin, was diagnosed with leukemia and that overshadowed everything. I really didn't get to enjoy *Bella Donna*. I found out that Robin was dying on the same day it went No. 1. I never really thought about it until now, but that's what happened. That should've been a time when I was the most happy and felt the most self-confident and successful. But actually, I really felt the most helpless, because all the money in the world couldn't save this woman's life. It was a very sad, yet balancing, thing for me. As a further complication, Robin was pregnant." With only three months to live it seemed impossible to save the baby. Robin was determined to give [her] husband, Kim, something to take forward from their relationship. As comfort for her best friend, Stevie took Robin to Hawaii for relaxation, sailing, and to enjoy all the memories. She had been in Stevie's life since she was fifteen.

By this time, Stevie's romantic partnership with Paul Fishkin had ended. She was especially frustrated with the inquisition she was getting during these stressful times but Paul seemed to understand. "For whatever reasons—which aren't important—my relationship with Paul stopped, he is the one man in my life that was truly good. Truly understood. I was in an emotional trauma all through that fifteen months. And he stood by and watched it, and was as much help as he could be. While the rest of the world questioned me constantly, including my very close friends. About everything."[13]

By October of 1982, Robin's condition had deteriorated. She was forced to have an emergency C-section to save her baby, and "Matthew" was born three months prematurely. Just five days later, at thirty-two years of age, Robin Anderson lost her battle with leukemia.

"It's the only friendship that I've ever had or…well, I'm not going to say ever will have. We just started out together at fifteen years old. She kind of walked me through life. And, as I questioned would there be life after Fleetwood Mac, I certainly questioned would there be life after Robin. Then I found that there is life after Robin, except that it's not the same, not near as special. There's a spirit gone, and that's why I'm really dedicated to this leukemia [benefit]. That's why I will do anything I have to do to make as much money to get rid of this disease as I can because I would really never want anyone to experience losing someone as beautiful as her in this horrible way.

"She [Robin] taught me how to sing. She taught me how to use my voice. She made very sure before she left this planet that I was all right, that my voice was all right. I don't have problems with my voice now, but I did and it took us years to fix it. Robin was one of those people [who] when she walked in the room everybody looked. She was breathtaking, and that's why it's so wild that she could possibly have died. It just doesn't make any sense at all."

During the final performance of the *Bella Donna* promotion tour, "White Wing Dove," a teary Stevie was forced to deal with the pain of separation yet again as she left the stage and thanked the audience. She had gained strength from her fans, but that onstage connection was over for awhile. She was back to coping with the loss of her best friend in other ways. Given her commitment to Fleetwood Mac, Stevie didn't take the time to grieve. She was on tour promoting the *Mirage* album and couldn't take any time off. Stevie became very emotional, bursting into tears when she would sing certain songs or hear something on the radio that triggered the pain. Her accelerating cocaine use didn't help matters, either.

While trying to keep her Fleetwood Mac colleagues satisfied and proceeding with her solo career, Stevie added another facet to her already chaotic life. Robin's husband, Kim Anderson, was the one person with whom she could really share the tragedy of Robin's death. As such, not long after the funeral, Stevie announced that she and Kim were getting married.

Her friends and family were in complete shock. "When Stevie passed thirty and had not gotten married," her father revealed for *Arizona Living* in 1983, "I honestly did not think she ever would. When a woman goes that long being single, and particularly when she's hugely successful, usually her career is so important that she won't get married. So at thirty-four, when she did get married, it was quite a shock to her mother and me.

"We met Kim a number of times when he was married to Robin. He's a very nice young man, but I can't say we were overly pleased with the marriage. Frankly, we felt that Stevie was possibly marrying Kim out of love for Robin and a feeling that somebody had to be a mother to a new baby. And we felt it was too early for her to marry Kim. Robin had been dead only four or five months. But she has tremendous intestinal fortitude and when she makes up her mind to do something, nobody can change it."

As further evidence of the codependent escape, they were married by the same minister who comforted Robin during her last days. The wedding, however, has been described as more of a fairytale. Stevie wore rose and lace and with her hair done in golden ringlets, looked like a fairy princess. Yet the marriage would end very soon. "We didn't get married because we were in love, we got married because we were grieving and it was the only way that we could feel like we were doing the right thing. And we got divorced three months later, and I haven't seen Kim, nor Matthew, since that day. I suppose that Matthew will find me when he's ready. I mean, I am, really, next to Robin, his mommy. But Kim and I can't deal with each other at all. So when the baby's old enough, I have all of his mother's things, and I have her life on film for fourteen, fifteen years. I have us on tape singing, I have a beautiful book that I wrote the year that she died...I have a roomful of stuff for him. I have his mother to give back to him when he's ready."14

After her brief marriage had ended, Stevie went back to her songwriting. Following in the footsteps of her grandfather, who'd lived in a trailer in the mountains, Stevie said she'd be just fine on a mountaintop with her typewriter and her piano. While working on Fleetwood Mac's *Mirage* album, she was also completing songs for her second solo album, *The Wild Heart*, which would be released in June of 1983 and dedicated to Robin Anderson. Stevie was spending less and less time in the studio with Fleetwood Mac, only going in when it was time to add her vocals or for mandatory band meetings. This continued to fuel the rumors that she was leaving the band.

"Stand Back," a top five hit in the United States, catapulted *The Wild Heart* up the charts. It was also a big dance club success, reaching number twelve on the Billboard dance charts and received a nomination for Best Rock Vocal Performance by a Female Artist at the 26th Annual Grammy Awards. On the *VH1 Storytellers* special, taped on August 18, 1998, at Sony Music Studios in New York, Stevie told the story of "Stand Back." She was driving with her husband Kim from Los Angeles to Santa Barbara for their honeymoon and heard Prince's "Little Red Corvette" on the radio. She began to sing along but with her own lyrics. When they got to the hotel, they recorded the demo tape.

In the middle of recording it at Sunset Sound in Los Angeles, she called Prince to tell him about her song. She hummed the song for him, and twenty minutes later he came roaring into the studio, listened to the song, played the synthesizer parts, and left. They did develop a friendship, but Stevie has said that Prince, being very straight laced, was not comfortable with her drug use and has also made it clear that they never had a sexual relationship. "I was sick, and Prince brought some cough syrup up to my hotel room. He was sweet—he walked around the room folding things, fluffing pillows, tidying up in general. Then he gave me a spoon of it himself. But when I asked for another spoonful he changed—he said, 'I didn't come all the way up here just to get you hooked on another substance!' Then he left."

When asked if she still sees him, she went on to say, "I was at the premiere of *Purple Rain*, and in the scene where he slaps Apollonia I freaked and had to go sit in the bathroom. Afterward I went back to see him, and when he asked why I'd left, I had to tell him, 'When you popped Apollonia, it kinda popped my brain.' He looked at me like it just killed him. We've never spoken since. It's a shame; really…we were alike in so many ways. Well, for one thing, we both liked wearing black chiffon around the house."[15]

The Wild Heart album cover was photographed by Herbert Worthington. He and Stevie came up with the concept together to depict the different parts of Stevie. At the far left of the cover, a crouching Stevie portrays her loneliness or sadness as the private side of her personality. At the far right is the strong Stevie, the performer, the star, the public image. The ghostly figure in the middle represents the spirit of the late Robin Anderson, who Stevie carries inside her wild heart always.

"It's like Bella Donna's heart is wild all of a sudden," she told *Rock* magazine. "It has that James Dean/Natalie Wood feeling to it. It's just *Bella Donna* a little more reckless. She's just surer of herself now, so she's taking a few more chances. I'm very pleased with the album because there are no holds barred on it. It's real strong and emotional. 'Sable in Blond' is my serious statement on *The Wild Heart*. It fits into a particular group of my songs; 'Rhiannon,' 'Beautiful Child' and 'Sara.' It reflects the mood I was in when I moved into my new house last year. It was a time when I was learning how to live with myself. 'Sable in Blond' meant to learn how to be a stranger, to learn to be with you, to learn to be one color. In the legend of Excalibur, the sword is there for protection, but you don't call upon it unless it's absolutely necessary. During that period in my life, I was learning how not to call on the sword."

"Nightbird" was another song written about her personal pain and loss, as she explained in *The Wild Heart* press kit. "This song does extend from 'Edge of Seventeen'; it's about the difficulties of female rock 'n' roll singers; it's about my friend Robin, it's about death, it's a spirit calling. Wearing boots all summer long is like, always being ready for a flood or avalanche to happen, for the worst to happen. Because when you really look at life, all the money, material things and dreams we all search after could not save one small girl." It was Stevie's hope that *The Wild Heart* and its dedication to Robin would stimulate more leukemia research.

The album enjoyed an eleven-week run in the top ten, and while the album went platinum, it did not reach the level of success of *Bella Donna*.

In fact, Christopher Connelly's review, "Trouble in Fantasyland, Stevie nixed," for *Rolling Stone* was harsh. He rated the album as fair and wondered how it had all turned out so badly. He described much of the record as an outright catastrophe, a one-two punch of cracked-cookie lyrics and stunningly pedestrian music, referring to the songs as inchoate ramblings. He went on to say that stanzas didn't hang together and choruses verged on the utterly meaningless. While "Enchanted" has evolved as one of Stevie's trademark tour songs, often kicking off her set, Mr. Connelly declared it could have made a nifty Warren Zeon song musically, but that it sounded ludicrous behind Stevie's "tinkerbell tales and arrhythmic count-off."

Steve Pond from the *Los Angeles Times* was just as antagonistic about the tour. "The imagery is predictable and shallow, her frequent dying-swan routines laughable, her barely coherent, giggle-laden comments embarrassing. But there's always a market for earnest silliness masquerading as poetic insight, and one look at the adoring fans who showered Nicks with roses and stuffed animals demonstrates how firmly she connects with her fans. She's not cynical or manipulative but apparently baffled and honestly touched by the emotion she inspires. All this doesn't make the spectacle any easier to enjoy, just harder to dismiss.

"And her honest, addle-headed lyrics are often backed by persuasive music. In a way, Nicks constantly rewrites the same songs, but her generic ballad has an attractive lilt to it, whether it's called 'Dreams' or 'Sara' or 'Gypsy' or 'Rhiannon' (her first hit and, as one friend of hers laughed, 'the Sisters of the Moon national anthem'). But Nicks has always been more attractive as part of a Fleetwood Mac show, where many of the best songs come while she's offstage changing veils. However hospitable her fans find Nicks's magic kingdom, she is simply too fluttery, flighty and silly to command a stage."

The second single, "If Anyone Falls," was only moderately successful. During a 1983 *MTV* interview, Stevie was asked about her collaborator on the album, Sandy Stewart. "Sandy is a little girl from Houston, Texas, who is an incredible writer and an incredibly funny, nice person. She and I wrote 'If Anyone Falls in Love.' A friend of mine gave me a tape of hers that I really didn't want to hear just as I was going into the studio. I was so inspired when I heard it, I wrote the lyrics to that and 'Nothing Ever Changes' that night. From that day onward, Sandy and I considered ourselves…kind of the Rodgers and Hammerstein of rock. If someone can write a track that I really love, I'll be glad to write a song to it, because I've got about 800,000 pages of words. I've never really written with anyone before. But now…we wrote 'Nightbird' in a couple of hours, sitting in my living room, with her synthesizer and me pacing. We don't have…an ego thing between the two of us, because we're so knocked out that there's someone who can do the other part, that each of us would rather not do. I think it's really neat that we have kind of established ourselves as a song-writing team, though—it's a wonderful new part of our lives."

The Wild Heart tour started in May of 1983 and went through November. Stevie went with four backup singers and Waddy Wachtel by her side on guitar. According to Mick Fleetwood, the wear and tear of touring and making multiple albums a year began to take its toll. "I think she suffered physically a lot. She was running two gigs and two lives, separate lives that were equally as powerful, and it took a hell of a lot out of her to retain that loyalty to Fleetwood Mac and not go, 'See ya.' I think it was quite devastating for her."[16]

Stevie in the early '80s
(Photo by Sam Emerson)

Stevie with Kenny Loggins in 1978
(Chris Walter / Photofeatures)

Stevie with Tom Petty in 1981
(© Scott Weiner / Retna Ltd.)

Stevie with Robin Snyder Anderson
(Source: VHI: Behind the Music)

Stevie in 1981
(Chris Walter / Photofeatures)

Stevie Nicks—Glen Helen Regional Park, CA, U.S. Festival, May 20, 1983
(*© Roger Ressmeyer / CORBIS*)

Stevie in 1983
(Chris Walter / Photofeatures)

Stevie with Jimmy Iovine—
10th Annual American Music
Awards, Shrine Auditorium, Los
Angeles, CA, January 17, 1983
(Ron Galella / WireImage)

Stevie in 1983
(Chris Walter / Photofeatures)

Stevie with Kim Anderson—Launch party for the
1st Annual Rock-N-Run Concert Tour, Canard de
Bombay Restaurant, Beverly Hills, CA, March 22, 1983
(Ron Galella / WireImage)

Five

Fleetwood Mac in France—
The *Mirage* Album

Following the completion of *Bella Donna* in early 1981, Stevie joined the rest of Fleetwood Mac at LeChateau, a recording studio outside Paris where Elton John recorded *Honky Chateau*. Production was handled by Fleetwood Mac together with Richard Dashut and Ken Caillat, the team responsible for the *Rumours* album. "We're closing in on it," Stevie told *The Record*. "It's very Rumouresque. I hate to use that word, but it is." Despite the demands from the release of *Bella Donna* and Robin's battle with leukemia, she contributed three songs to the album.

Her contributions included "Straight Back," "That's Alright," and "Gypsy"—the latter a song that's particularly close to her heart. "That's Alright" began as a demo entitled "Designs of Love." Stevie apparently tried to get the song on each of the three prior Fleetwood Mac albums before *Mirage*, but to no avail. The collective intelligence of the group did not see the song as a fit with the sound and feel of earlier albums.

"Gypsy" is in some ways the "Rhiannon" of the eighties. It evokes so many different emotions. The song was originally written for *Bella Donna* but was used for *Mirage* instead. Stevie has attributed "Gypsy" to her pre-stardom, hippie days in San Francisco when she used to wait in line for hours outside the Fillmore Auditorium and fantasize about what it would be like to be a star and arrive at the Fillmore in a big black limousine. "In basic ways, I haven't changed. In material ways, of course, I've changed a lot. Because I'm not starving now and I don't have to worry where my rent's coming from and that makes it a lot easier on my blood pressure. I still love all the same things.

"Every place I live still looks pretty much like my apartment in San Francisco. The clothes I wear…that doesn't change. I love long dresses. I love velvet. I love high boots. I never change. I love the same eye make-up. I'm not a fad person. I still have everything I had then. That's one part of me…That's where my songs come from. There's a song on the new *Fleetwood Mac* album that says, 'Going back to the velvet underground/Back to the floor that I love,' because I always put my bed on the floor." She quotes from the song again. 'To a room with some lace and paper flowers/Back to the gypsy that I was.' And that's San Francisco. That's the velvet underground. Those are the things that I can't give up."[1]

"I think 'Gypsy' was one of my best collaborations ever with Stevie…in terms of what I do for Stevie as far as arrangement and things go," Lindsey told *Guitar World*. "I think that was one of the most effective pieces we've ever done."

"I still see your bright eyes, bright eyes," was, according to Stevie, written in memory of her friend Robin. Stevie was saying that even though Robin was gone, she felt her presence no matter where she was or what she was doing in her life.

With the success Stevie experienced as a result of her triple platinum solo album, *Bella Donna*, speculation and rumor fueled the release of *Mirage*. By this time, she was spending less and less time in the studio in favor of her own projects, and everyone seemed to know it. The press was consumed with Stevie's intentions to continue with Fleetwood Mac. She demonstrated her ambivalence in "Straight Back." The song compared working with Fleetwood Mac and having a solo career.

The band's resentment began to show in interviews. Lindsey, Mick, and Christine were openly antagonistic about Stevie's lack of commitment to Fleetwood Mac while speaking with David Gans at *The Record*. Lindsey, in his typically direct manner, explained, "She's flexing some kind of emotional muscles that she feels she can flex now that she's in a more powerful position. There's a certain amount of leeway in how you can interpret Stevie's behavior, I'd say, but at the same time there's no denying that her success is making her feel that she can pull things that she wouldn't have felt comfortable pulling before. And most of them aren't particularly worthwhile, but she's venting something—loneliness, unhappiness or something."

Adding fuel to the fire, David Gans had this to say about Stevie's songwriting abilities. "In spite of the overwhelming success of her solo album, there is a certain, well amateurish quality to Nicks' songs. The way she lays a lyric across a melody sometimes makes for awkward phrasing and contributes to the spaciness of her musical persona, as does her rather childish lyrical point of view regarding life and love."

Even Christine had had something to say. "Stevie's very prolific. She writes constantly, and all her songs are like babies to her even though some of them are rubbish. When I write, I sit down and work on an idea until it's finished, but Stevie cranks out songs all the time."

Speaking about how playing music together as a band was gratifying for everyone but Stevie, Lindsey speculated. "That may have something to do with why Stevie is the way she is now. Because she is not a musician, she doesn't share in that thing with us. She can feel totally out of her depth—which she is, on some levels—and you can understand why she doesn't want to come down to the studio or be involved in certain things."

"She phones her part in," Christine said without an ounce of irony. "She asks what songs we plan on doing and what songs we want her to do. The rest of it will be decided between Mick, Lindsey and me."[2] What is interesting, however, is that none of the band members seemed to know what Stevie wanted to do. Even Mick Fleetwood couldn't keep track of her intentions. "I'm sure at times she wants to go off and not be a part of the band, and at other times it's the opposite." This level of examination and criticism was something Stevie had not experienced since early in her Fleetwood Mac tenure. She'd always been proud of her philosophical songwriting abilities and, given her sensitive nature, found such public antagonism very hurtful.

It didn't help that Lindsey, in the same interview with David Gans, publicly praised his collaboration with Christine McVie. "She and I have a real valid kind of rapport between us…something that was there before we even met. It's like she can play the piano and I can play the guitar just wonderfully along with her. It's almost like parallel lines during our formative years of music until we met, and it gave us a lot of common ground."

Christine does admit that Stevie hasn't always been welcome in the studio. "There've been many times when she might come out in the studio and try and sing along, and we'd tend to say, 'Don't do that right now, let us work this out first.' Now she'll just go to the studio and go, 'There's no need for me to be here.' She does feel left out."

Even Stevie has spoken of her disconnection from the band. "I'm not one of the players and that puts me on the other side of the mirror; alone, with them out in the studio. It's very lonely."[3] She elaborated further. "I love the way Fleetwood Mac sounds. I wouldn't be in it if I didn't. But I just didn't want to devote quite so much time to *Bella Donna*, because I'm too lazy. On *Tusk* I was at the studio almost every day for thirteen months but I probably only worked for two months. The other eleven I did nothing, and you start to lose your mind after a while if you're not active. See, they all play instruments and I don't. So I'm looking at them through a window in the studio; five hours go by and they don't even remember I'm there. It's frustrating."[4] This painful theme lived on in the name of her 1989 solo album, *The Other Side of the Mirror*.

Stevie performing in 1982
(© Lynn Goldsmith / CORBIS)

Stevie performing—1980s
(© Photorazzi)

Stevie with Christine McVie
(Source: www.nicksfix.com)

Six

Rock a Little and *The Other Side of the Mirror*

In 1985, Stevie and Jimmy Iovine went back to the studio to record Stevie's third solo album, *Rock A Little*. But her cocaine addiction had escalated and was affecting her performance to such a degree that Iovine eventually reached his level of tolerance and quit the project, leaving Stevie's self-destructive behavior far behind.

"I think it got to a point with Jimmy and I, where, I really just got a little bit too crazy. It wasn't any fun for him anymore, you know, and I understood that. It wasn't hard to understand, why he wouldn't want to do it anymore."[1]

In an interview with Mary Turner for *Off the Record*, Stevie defined the album's title. "Rock a little means perseverance—rock a little means rock a little all the time. If you rock out, you may not rock any more." Stevie was clearly not living within her own self-advised boundaries.

Her producer from the Buckingham Nicks days, Keith Olsen, replaced Iovine at the helm. Nevertheless, Stevie's persistent cocaine use along with early recording issues delayed the album's release from its originally scheduled date of late 1984 until November of 1985. The album spawned three singles: "Talk to Me," "I Can't Wait," and "Has Anyone Ever Written Anything For You," and ultimately reached number twelve on the Billboard charts. Indeed, it was eventually certified platinum.

But despite Olsen's best efforts, *Rock A Little* ultimately garnered the same negative critical reaction as its predecessor, *The Wild Heart*. A *Rolling Stone* review of the album began, "Nicks slips out of touch. The sensitive rock artiste, making self-indulgent solo statements in a vacuum, supposedly died out in the late Seventies. The real shame is that Nicks could make a good record again, if she'll only take her advice and rock a little."

Even the *San Francisco Chronicle* got in on the action. A scathing concert review by Joel Selvin included the following painful quips: "Performing under the tent top that someone has said looks like the world's biggest brassiere, Nicks sounded as if she had ground off the top half of her vocal range, growling and rasping her way through a listless and ineffective performance. The former lead vocalist of Fleetwood Mac still boasts an enormously loyal following, more than 10,000 strong Monday, a crowd littered with young women dressed in quirky layers of lace like Nicks. She clearly strikes a heartfelt chord with her fans. But to her more discriminating admirers, what a disappointment the show must have been. Three background vocalists covered the high notes for Nicks, who seems to have lost power as well as range in her singing. She treated the crowd to a program of pop-rock specialties from her solo albums, interspersing a few oldies from the big Mac, but emphasizing selections from her latest LP, which spawned the big hit, *I Can't Wait*.

"Her crack band functioned flawlessly, if a bit heavily on the bottom end of the massive sound, wrapping her vocals in an alternately billowing and thunderous cloud," Selvin continued. "Ever the eccentric diva, Nicks danced absentmindedly between vocals, dropping into deep knee bends and skipping off the stage for frequent costume changes. She gushed about her early days in the South Bay with former paramour and Mac associate Lindsey Buckingham. ("We opened for everybody.") The precious poetic content of her lyrics read more like Hallmark than Dylan Thomas, but the romantic soap operas she spins obviously find their mark with her audience."

On *VH1 Storytellers,* Stevie proclaimed that "Has Anyone Ever Written Anything For You" is probably her most intense song. It was spurred on by an event during *The Wild Heart* tour in 1984, where Joe Walsh opened for her and became her close friend and love interest. At the time, Stevie was feeling quite anxious over a personal matter, and Walsh felt it was important in the scheme of their lives to help her rise above it. When they arrived in Denver, Colorado, he rented a jeep and drove her to Boulder, where he told her a story of a little girl who was killed in a car accident on her way to nursery school. It was his little girl, and it all happened right there in Boulder.

Walsh took Stevie to a nearby park and walked with her to a small, silver drinking fountain. A plaque on the fountain read, "To Emma Kristen, for all those who can't, or aren't big enough to get a drink." Something about this story touched Stevie so deeply that she immediately went home to Phoenix, got out of her car, walked to the Bosendorfer piano in her front entryway, sat down, and wrote the song. Stevie has often described Walsh as her soulmate. "We were busy being superstars and everyone was doing way too many drugs. But I was so in love with him. Joe is married again, but we're still close."[2] "Sister Honey" was recorded at Stevie's home with esteemed guitarist, Les Dudek, and was inspired by their friendship.

"Rock A Little" was written before *Bella Donna* was released. Stevie has said it was prompted by the sound of the ocean waves that seemed to shake her house, scaring her to death every night. She thought it sounded like an earthquake. "Even when it's calm the house still shook a little/Just like the sea I rock a little/Some say it was just like me—Rock a little. That means cool out. Relax. Okay. Just rock a little all the time and you won't die."[3]

In April of 1986, Stevie began a four-month tour in the United States to support the record. She also performed several shows in Australia, her first concerts as a solo artist outside the United States. During the tour, her cocaine use exploded. Her audience witnessed an embarrassing fall onstage in Houston, Texas, and she experienced frequent nosebleeds between shows.

Paul Fishkin remembered how bad things got for Stevie. "There were times when we had to just scrape her off the floor. [She had] near overdoses on the road."[4] *USA Today,* on April 14, 1986, reported her fall in Houston. "At the end of several numbers, she crouched at the stage's edge to grasp outstretched hands. Reaching out to the audience led to a tense moment late in the show, when Nicks fell, apparently into a hole at the stage's side. Crew members lifted her to her feet, and she returned to the microphone for two encores. After 'Has Anyone Ever Written Anything for You,' she bid a fond farewell: 'Stay well for me and be here for me when I come back. And I love you more than anything.'"

By June of 1986, Stevie's onstage antics were being compared to Elvis's. Daniel Brogan provided a brutally honest account of her concert in the *Chicago Tribune.* "The evening's headliner, on the other hand, is riding an expressway to creative oblivion and self-destruction.

"Stevie Nicks, who with Fleetwood Mac topped Frampton in the sales record books, followed the guitar player with a collection of her Fleetwood Mac and solo hits that provided a graphic picture of what bad shape she is in. Years of hard living have reduced her voice to a wretched rasp that no longer even tries to hit the high notes. Instead, she spent much of her 90-minute set spinning and whirling on and off the stage, often leaving her bewildered-looking band to pick up the pieces.

"She began the evening wrapped in a blue cape that looked like a bed-spread at grandma's house. Midway in the set, however, she removed the bedspread and revealed that her voice is not the only thing that's gotten away from her.

"As the show progressed, Nicks seemed increasingly disoriented and her offstage jaunts grew in frequency and length. She ended the evening with a declaration of love for the audience that was as rambling and incoherent as any late—'70s Elvis monologue. Maybe that's an apt comparison."

Still in denial, Stevie went to her doctor to receive treatment for the nosebleeds. He looked at her nose and told her she could have a brain hemorrhage. She realized she was going to have to end the habit she'd had since 1977 or it would kill her. "Eventually, I was working so hard that I lost the belief that I could carry on without them."[5]

The last time Stevie used cocaine was just before going onstage during a concert at Red Rocks, Colorado, in 1986, a show that symbolically ended with the release of twenty-five white doves. One of the birds refused to leave Stevie's hand so she kept it as a pet. To explain her legacy for some-one who is unaware of her rock star status, she has said she would put on her Red Rocks concert video and let them absorb the vastness and rock 'n' roll atmosphere of that beautiful venue.

Not long after the show, she went to the Betty Ford Clinic and has not used cocaine since. The close-up shots for the video release had to be re-shot at a time when she wasn't so high. "I would never lecture anybody because I don't think that's the way to get to people. It certainly wasn't the way to get to me. I decided to go to Betty Ford. Nobody came and threw me in a van and took me. That was my decision. I booked the room. I paid for it. So I really think when it comes down to that stuff, it's really all up to you."[6] True to Stevie's metaphorical approach to writing and speaking, she described for *USA Today* how cocaine had ruled her. "It was like being swept up on a white horse by a prince. There was no way to get off the white horse and I didn't want to. It took over my life in a big way."

While Stevie has described her decision to go to Betty Ford as purely vol-untary, Mick Fleetwood told a slightly different story in his autobiography. He recalled an intervention from family and friends as being the impetus for treatment after she fell off the stage during the *Rock a Little* tour.

In 1988, Linda Romine of *Cox News Service* reported Stevie's father's recollection. "After repeated attempts to help her, we flew to Los Angeles one night and convinced her to enter the Betty Ford Center in California. She resisted it when we confronted her with it," Stevie's father said. "She was concerned...that it would be publicized and be detrimental to her career. We spent most of the night with her and convinced her though, that it was for her health. Finally, she said, 'OK, Daddy, I'll do it.'

"It's tough. It's really tough," he said, shaking his head. "Christ, the career means nothing to the parents when it comes to the health of your children."

Stevie Nicks remembered her parents' lifesaving intervention from a different perspective. "He basically said to me, 'How could you possibly even consider putting me through not having you for the rest of my life?'", she recalled quietly. "He said, 'Do you have any idea what it would do to me if you weren't around? You may be a rock 'n' roll star to the rest of the world, but you are still my daughter, and if you were to die…'" Overcome with emotion, she could not continue the sentence.

After 28 days at the Betty Ford Center, Stevie was determined to turn her life around. And she has.

"It is scary. It is frightening," she explained. "But I walked out of those doors saying to myself, 'I'm gonna win this. I'm not gonna disappoint my dad. I'm not going to break his heart.'"

"I was one chain-smoking, coffee-swilling mess while I was there [at Betty Ford]. And I ate like a pig—they feed you way up for the other stuff you are suddenly missing. And I cried a lot. You don't have treatment as such but meetings with your counselor and with everyone together. You cry and you cry and you tell all your secret stories. In three days you are out of pain and crying for a purpose. You are hopeful, but never really happy."[7]

It was through her experience in rehabilitation that she learned new coping mechanisms and realized she didn't have to be superwoman. "So when I went to Betty Ford, I realized that cocaine allowed me to do more than it was necessary for me to do. The important things I had to do got done anyway. And all that extra time allowed me to do a bunch of stuff not that well. You know, like you get crazy and say well, I'm just gonna write three songs tonight, I'm gonna sit at my typewriter and I'm gonna write ten pages of my future book, and I'm gonna go through my closets and I'm gonna pick out all the things that I want to take with me on my next trip. I'm gonna do all that by tomorrow. And you don't have to do that. What I learned at Betty Ford is that it isn't necessary to go non-stop, seven days a week, even though everybody will always tell you that."[8] One of her homework assignments was to write an essay on the difference between Stevie Nicks the real-life person and Stevie Nicks the rock star. "A tough one," she told *Raw* in June of 1989. Stevie's identity, for many years, was completely linked to her rock star status.

"What did it for me," she told *You*, "was seeing so many people in much worse shape than me. I had three men friends in their 60s, all rich, all from Texas who sat down and told me the stories of their lives. How they'd had it all and lost it, betrayed their family and friends and businesses and destroyed their own and everyone else's lives. One by one they would look at me with tears running down their faces and say: 'Stevie, don't do this to your life.' They all helped me make the most important resolution of my life: that I will not be 65 years old and be in Betty Ford."

"Considering the generation we come from, we are very lucky to be alive. When you have to sit down and write on a piece of paper, 'I am not special. I am dying,' that's a real serious thing to swallow. And that's one of the things you have to write down there [at Betty Ford]. You finally reach a point where you say, 'I am rich. I am famous. I have everything I want and I am dying.' That's about as serious as it can get."9

In an interview with *The Guardian*, Stevie got quite graphic about the lasting effects of her and Christine McVie's heavy cocaine use. "Here," she said, "give me your pen. [She makes a little sketch of two noses.] That's the hole in Chris's nose and that's the hole in my nose. [The first is a tiny dot, the other the size of a dime.] You could put a big gold ring through my septum. It affects my eyes, my sinuses. It was a lot of fun for a long time, because we didn't know it was bad. But eventually it gets hold of you and all you can think about is where your next line is coming from." She has chosen not to get her septum repaired because it would change her trademark voice.

Stevie's drug abuse reached such incomparable levels that rumors arose about her mode of delivery. Her nose reportedly damaged, it was believed that she had an assistant deliver the cocaine using alternative methods. A myth Stevie wholeheartedly denies despite being called the "Queen of the Stoned Age" by *Q magazine* as recently as May 2001.

While talking with Jenny Boyd, Mick Fleetwood's first wife, for Jenny's book, *Musicians in Tune*, Stevie helped her understand what it's been like since getting clean. "I think a lot of us realize we're really lucky to be alive. The ones of us who did make it pretty much cherish the fact that we are alive. You have to learn if you can't depend on yourself without [chemicals], you might as well stop doing it and go do something else, because it isn't worth dying for…But it is difficult, and probably always will be difficult to accept this whole life in a different way…Because for so long it was lived under that dream cloud, dream child world of different kinds of drugs."

"Let's get one thing straight, cocaine is not a creative drug! If you take cocaine it will not help you to create a masterpiece. But what it will do is help you to put the tiredness at the back of your mind. If you've worked all hours, six days solid and you have to face another day under that kind of pressure, you might think that some sort of stimulant is going to be the answer. But I didn't know about cocaine until I was 29, and let me tell you this; Fleetwood Mac never dabbled in heroin. We never wanted to commit suicide. OK, so pop stars do cocaine, but then so do lots of other people. If all the money spent on cocaine was spent on conservation instead, we could repair the hole in the ozone layer, clean up all the rivers and re-plant all the rain forests that have been destroyed."[10]

"I haven't done cocaine for eight years," she told Lance Loud of *Details* in 1994. "Unfortunately, it's just the way I have to live. Do I miss it? Yeah, I miss it. Would I ever do it again? No. The doctors told me that I'd have a brain hemorrhage if I drank or did drugs."

"What makes me angry with myself is that a whole lot of money went out for that, which we all could have in our bank accounts right now. Like, I lost a very good friend to leukemia about six years ago. And at this point in my life, I wish I had all that money to give to leukemia research."[11]

Since Stevie has removed all the dangerous substances from her body, things are much better. "I am happy. I want you to really know that. I really do love what I do and this is the first time since before Fleetwood Mac that I can say I feel like that same girl who joined Fleetwood Mac. There aren't all the drugs. I have a shot of tequila before I go on stage, but that's it. I don't drink after the show. I don't carry that on with me so my life is pretty clear now and I'm really enjoying it."[12]

Realizing how her drugging was perceived, she admits that partying is not in her best interest. "Well, there's a little bit of the attitude that if you don't go and party, you're kind of out of the loop. But, you know, it's sure nice to wake up and have somebody hand you the *New York Times* and have a really good review in it, instead of everybody going "Oh, God."[13]

In early 1988, Stevie hit the wall. Having pushed herself to the point of exhaustion, she was diagnosed with Epstein-Barr, a viral-induced chronic fatigue syndrome. It was diagnosed after her silicon breast implants were removed. "They [breast implants] made me very sick," she somberly told *Australian Woman's Weekly*. "I had them done in December 1976. I'd only been in Fleetwood Mac one year and I was getting a lot of attention. I had always thought my hips were too big and I had no chest. I reckoned it would look better on stage, but I'd advise against having them. They will backfire. You will have to take them out and that leaves you scarred. I had terrible bouts of Epstein-Barr syndrome after they were removed. I was in and out of the hospital, at the doctor's three times a week, taking acupuncture, having IVs to clean the toxic silicone out of my body. It was truly awful."

"Once you've had it [Epstein-Barr], you have it, always. But I don't have [the symptoms] right now. If you get all depressed and bummed out and worn out, it comes back. I had it for two years. I tried acupuncture. I took vitamins. I did everything. Then one day it just went away. It has a lot to do with your state of mind."[14]

The *Tango in the Night* tour had spanned four months, but the final few shows were canceled due to her illness as Mick recalled. "She had a battle with that [Epstein-Barr] for years as far as I remember. No one would understand, you can't be that tired. Well, your sleeping all the time, you know. Of course she's sleeping all the time, she's ill."[15] As she does when in need of comfort, Stevie retreated to her home in Paradise Valley. To recover from her chronic fatigue syndrome, she allowed herself some much-needed rest for the next year.

In 1989 Stevie was back and ready to rock. She was healthy and poised to make her fourth solo album. Stevie rented a Dutch-style castle for $25,000 a month in Los Angeles and transformed the dining room into a recording studio. She has called *The Other Side of the Mirror* her magic album. Had she just transferred her addiction to another excess?

The first track from Stevie's fourth solo album, produced by Rupert Hines, was "Rooms on Fire," a song that eventually turned out to be Stevie's biggest hit ever in Europe. Then came the duet with Bruce Hornsby called "Two Kinds of Love," the song written during her tour with Bob Dylan and Tom Petty and one to which Kenny G also contributed.

The third single, "Whole Lotta Trouble," was released in the United States. It was recorded by Michael Campbell at Lionshare Studio. Stevie was thrilled to have the LA Horns, who happened to be in the studio, perform the brass parts rather than relying on the typical synthesizer approach. An additional single, "Long Way To Go," was released in Europe and Japan, and Bruce Hornsby played piano on "Juliet."

The album's name came from the song "Alice" and was meant to encompass Stevie's life between Fleetwood Mac, her solo work, painting, and blanket making. Alice was her grandmother's name. Stevie called her "Crazy Alice," but sadly she died before the record was released. Stevie referred to her death as "really on the other side of the mirror."

Stevie's description of what inspired the first single on the album makes the song quite real. "I guess the single ["Rooms on Fire"] is about when you're in a crowded room and you see a kind of person who makes your heart go 'wow!' The whole world seems to be ablaze at that particular moment. You see, I don't write fantasy songs. Everything I write is based on personal experience. I guess I'm quite an intense, romantic person. Of course, selling lots of records means you can live a privileged, glamorous lifestyle, but it becomes very lonely as well."[16]

Stevie revealed the inspiration for "Has Anyone Ever Written Anything for You" more clearly in her liner notes from the *Timespace* album as she described meeting Joe Walsh. "I guess in a very few rare cases…some people find someone that they fall in love with the very first time they see them…from across a room, from a million miles away. Some people call it love at first sight, and of course, I never believed in that until…that night…I walked into a party after a gig at the hotel, and from across the room, without my glasses I saw this man…and I walked straight to him…He held out his hands to me, and I walked straight into them. I remember thinking, I can never be far from this person again…he is my soul."

"Fire Burning" exemplifies Stevie's fear of fires. She had experienced two fires in her life, one at age six and another when she was twenty-nine or thirty, during which she grabbed her dog, cashmere blanket, tapes, music, and semi-precious jewels and fled from the house. "Doing the Best I Can" was written as an autobiographic representation of where Stevie saw herself at the time. As she explained in *Reflections from the Other Side of the Mirror*, "Long Way to Go" was written in October of 1985, after her ex-boyfriend had summoned her to his home and broke up with her all over again, thereby propelling her into another crying marathon. "I thought we already did that!" she shouted. They'd broken up a year before. Who was Stevie dating in 1984? Joe Walsh.

During the tour supporting her new album, however, Stevie still didn't feel quite right. She was taking Klonopin, a tranquilizer prescribed for her to alleviate any further withdrawal symptoms from her cocaine detoxification. But now she had another chemical dependence, this time on a prescription drug.

This was a very painful time in Stevie's life—a time when she didn't care about anything and felt the fatigue of her new drug. She has since gained strength in sharing the experience. "Klonopin is like taking a lot of Valium; you want to get in your chair with your clicker and watch TV," she told Stephanie Tuck at *In Style* magazine.

The Other Side of the Mirror
Tour—1989
(Photo by Bill Paustenbach)

The Other Side of the Mirror
Tour—1989
(Photo by Bill Paustenbach)

Seven

Tango in the Night—The End of *Rumours*

In 1986, Lindsey Buckingham was getting ready to release what would have been his third solo album. However, the other members of Fleetwood Mac weren't having any of it. Ultimately, his songs appeared on the band's 1987 release, *Tango in the Night*.

Following her thirty-day cocaine treatment program at Betty Ford, Stevie vowed to stay clean but insisted on continuing her highly challenging career. As such, she immediately went into the studio to record *Tango in the Night*, Fleetwood Mac's fifth album since she and Lindsey joined the band. The album made it to the top ten on the U.S. charts and reached number one in Europe, an accomplishment both *Tusk* and *Mirage* had not achieved. Stevie's songs were "Welcome to the Room...Sara," "When I See You Again," and "Seven Wonders."

"Welcome to the Room...Sara" was clearly a depiction of her time at Betty Ford. She described the experience as "its not home and it's not Tara." Frontline, her management company at the time, was rumored to have given her an ultimatum and demanded she seek help for her out-of-control cocaine addiction. Speaking angrily, she sang, "You can take all the credit" and "Of course it was a problem."

Sandy Stewart wrote "Seven Wonders." Because Stevie had listened to the song only a few times before recording it, the line "all the way down you held the line" was recorded as "All the way down to Emmeline." "When I See You Again" was recorded before she was admitted to Betty Ford and when she sounded like a desperately sad woman. Stevie was on a path to self-destruction, a premise that can be heard in every note of the song.

Stevie didn't spend much time in the studio, preferring to record most of her vocals alone. Not surprisingly, the other members resented her for it. "I wasn't there for a lot of that [recording of *Tango in the Night*], 'cause I was on the road. It was me that was causing all the friction, 'cause Lindsey was the head guy and I was making him erratic. When I was not there it was good. They all got along fine. But, you have to understand that I'm an old girlfriend of Lindsey's, so that kind of makes me a war monger in his eye. So, when I walked in it was like, 'Thanks so much for stopping by. We heard you were busy with your solo tour. Thanks for bailing on us.' That's the first thing I got.

"I didn't have time for that abuse. And I felt like, 'If you don't get off my back, I'm gonna injure you badly.' It got so bad that I said, 'I'm gonna do a solo record,' much to Mick and Lindsey's absolute horror. From that moment on, I got treated much worse. However, they couldn't be too awful to me, 'cause they knew that they couldn't go out on the road without me. So they had to keep a certain level of niceness. Otherwise they knew I'd walk. I mean, I had platinum records and sold-out tours. Why did I need to be treated like this? There was plenty of jealousy in the air, but I felt so beaten down that I wanted to run away and hide."[1]

When she heard the final recordings, Stevie was very upset that she hadn't been asked to sing harmony on many of the songs. She didn't think the album even sounded like Fleetwood Mac. The other band members, frustrated that she'd decided against coming into the studio, nevertheless acquiesced and dubbed her vocals onto the record.

An expansive U.S. and European tour followed the album's release, but Lindsey backed out at the eleventh hour and left the band. Thusly, the amazing *Rumours* line-up came to an end.

It was the first time since 1975 that Fleetwood Mac would go on the road without Lindsey. "First he was going to the tour, and then he changed his mind, which of course made it awkward for the rest of us," Mick told *Music Express.* "I suggested Billy Burnett and Rick Vito whom I'd worked with, and we brought them into the rehearsals. They played four or five songs and someone in the room yelled out. 'Yeah! You're in!'"

"They were scared. They didn't try out. We just picked them and we went into rehearsal," Stevie said. "They were instantly part of the band. You can't be in Fleetwood Mac and be a side man. It must be a group, a band."[2] Despite Stevie's periodic feelings of alienation, she did realize the importance of working collectively as a band. After all, it was Lindsey being replaced, a key Fleetwood Mac figure and one that audiences revered.

The son of fifties musician Dorsey Burnette, Billy had toured and recorded with Mick's side band project, Zoo, and had co-written "So Excited" with Christine McVie, a song that appeared on her 1984 solo album. Rick Vito made his initial acquaintance with the band by recording with John McVie and blues legend John Mayall in the mid-seventies.

The fact that two people were needed to replace Lindsey Buckingham has not gone unnoticed by Lindsey or anyone who has followed Fleetwood Mac's highs and lows. Even Billy Burnette praised Lindsey's talent. "I have to say that playing Lindsey's songs made me appreciate how great a player he really is. For him to play those arrangements live by himself was no mean feat."[3]

Fleetwood Mac also released its *Greatest Hits* album in 1988 that included Stevie's new song, "No Questions Asked."

Stevie with Mick Fleetwood—1987
(Chris Walter / Photofeatures)

Stevie performing in the '80s
(© Henry Diltz / CORBIS)

Eight

Inaugurations and Reunions—Fleetwood Mac (1990s)

On the heels of Stevie's fourth solo album, the Fleetwood Mac *Tango in the Night* tour line-up released *Behind the Mask* in 1990. It received mixed reviews. Stevie honored her commitment and contributed four songs to the album.

Without Mick Fleetwood's friendship and ability to influence Stevie, she may not have participated at all. "Oh I've been close to leaving Fleetwood Mac ever since I joined Fleetwood Mac," Stevie told *Us*. "But so has everybody else. To be in Fleetwood Mac is to live in a soap opera. And it has been pretty scandalous and pretty incestuous, and pretty wonderful in a lot of ways."

But it just wasn't the same without Lindsey. The tour, which followed the release of the album, was the longest in the history of Fleetwood Mac. It took the band from Australia to the States, over to Europe and then back to North America.

This was Stevie's last album with Fleetwood Mac until their 1997 reunion. The *Behind the Mask* album and tour were completed during the "Klonopin years," when Stevie's energy and creativity were significantly impaired by the tranquilizing effect of the drug she was prescribed after leaving Betty Ford. Regardless, she made it through, only to face tougher years ahead.

After completing the tour for her solo album *The Other Side of the Mirror*, Stevie chose not to work on another Fleetwood Mac album. It was rumored to be a decision made because Stevie didn't like what Mick wrote about her in his autobiography. Apparently, it was because Warner Brothers would not allow Stevie to use Fleetwood Mac's version of "Silver Springs" on her soon-to-be-released *Timespace* album and she believed it was Mick's decision. Although Stevie wrote the song, she didn't have the authority to release it. The remaining members of Fleetwood Mac toyed with idea of finding another female vocalist but they didn't do it. They knew Stevie and her trademark voice were irreplaceable.

Stevie had sworn never to perform with Mick Fleetwood again, but the *Rumours* line-up reunited in 1993 for President Bill Clinton's inaugural ball. They were asked to play once more at Clinton's farewell party in 2001, but this time did so without Christine McVie since she'd already moved back to England. They performed the Mac classic "Don't Stop." Stevie has said she could not have felt more special, knowing they were out there because Bill Clinton wanted them.

"What was even more amazing was getting Lindsey on stage with the four of us again," Stevie quipped. "It took the President of the United States to do that. We all didn't think Lindsey would do it. I called him and said, 'If you cheat me out of this honoring moment, I'll never speak to you again.' So he did it."[1]

Stevie remembered giving President Clinton quite a scare. "One thing that sticks out about that performance is something nobody saw, because it was edited out. We were playing the song, and Mr. Clinton walked up on the stage to join us. I started to move toward him, and he got this terrified look on his face like, 'Oh my God, Stevie Nicks is coming toward me, and this is being watched by 18 million people.' He looked so terrified and uncomfortable that I just handed him my tambourine and said, 'Go to it, Mr. President.' And he did—he rocked out."[2]

After the performance, Stevie made the decision to leave Fleetwood Mac. "It was very hard to leave," she told Larry Katz of the *Boston Herald.* "I just couldn't leave them after Lindsey left in 1987. I couldn't do that to them, I just couldn't. But after Lindsey came and played the inauguration with us, I realized that I could never deal with Fleetwood Mac again unless it would be the five of us. And it will never be that way again. So I decided my part in that particular Shakespearean drama is over." Stevie has a pattern of making emphatic statements that ultimately require her to change her mind later when things have blown over.

In August of 1994, she was asked about her relationship with Lindsey. "He doesn't speak to me; we don't speak at all actually. He only played at the inauguration because I called him on the phone and begged him."[3] She further elaborated for Lance Loud of *Details.* "Christine and I will always be close; Lindsey just plain doesn't like me. I never had any musical training of any kind. I just had this innate ability to walk in, sit down at a piano, write a song in five minutes, and go to bed. It drives him nuts."

Fleetwood Mac fans had now been without their beloved band for several years. When asked about a possible reunion, she candidly responded, "I can't see [a reunion] happening. I'd have to feel them out. I could see Lindsey doing it if we offered some exorbitant amount of money. Me, personally...I would have to get a friendly, hopeful vibe from him, which usually isn't there. I don't need money that bad. It's not worth it."[4]

In May of 1996, with the *Rumours* twentieth anniversary approaching, Mick Fleetwood, Lindsey Buckingham, Christine and John McVie, and Stevie did reunite on stage for the Kentucky Derby in the Highlands home of local Louisville celebrity, Patricia Barnstable Brown. It was like old times with Mr. American Bandstand, Dick Clark, right in front of them.

In early 1997, it became apparent that the *Rumours* line-up reunion just wouldn't go away. It started with the 1997 reunion tour, a venture Buckingham was initially reluctant to do. While Mick Fleetwood was helping Lindsey Buckingham with his latest attempt at a solo album, the band stepped in again for what Buckingham told *Rocky Mountain News* in 2004 was "probably the most blatant form of what you might call an intervention-type situation. We actually had a dinner at Christine's [McVie] house where people after dinner got in a circle around me and said, 'You gotta do this thing.' I'm going, 'Oh my God, this is bizarre.'" Band members were contacted by *MTV* for a television special. The show was recorded at the Warner Brothers Studios in Fairbank, California, on May 22 and 23.

Stevie and Christine admitted to being very nervous about the event. *Mojo magazine* captured the product of such anxiety in their September 1997 interview with Stevie. "When "The Chain" is finished and the audience whoop, a familiar opening riff begins, and all eyes turn to Stevie Nicks, dressed in her trademark black chiffon. For one who has in recent years waxed matronly, she looks oddly like, well, Stevie Nicks. And then it happens. Stevie sings the opening line to "Dreams"…and forgets the words. It is the only Number 1 single in her life—maybe her most important song ever—and she flubs it. She stops—this is TV, remember—and starts over. And then she flubs it again.

"It is a tense moment. Some in the audience giggle, nervously. Others silently speculate on whether a refresher visit to the Betty Ford Clinic might be in order. But the moment passes. Stevie finally nails it, and Fleetwood Mac, as the saying goes, Then Play On."

"You know what?" Stevie asked Dave DiMartino at *Mojo magazine* "I wasn't pissed off at myself, I was scared—the words went out of my head. The first time it was like, OK, this is all right. The second time I started to get a sick feeling. And then the third time I thought, Somebody, *Lindsey*, come over here and tell me these words, because we're not gonna get *through* this thing.

"But," she added, "also I'm thinking, the audience is really gonna *enjoy* this—they're gonna see that I *too* am stupid and an airhead, and things go wrong for me too, and everything isn't perfect. And they're gonna not have a problem with it."

Stevie's voice on *The Dance* album and tour was stronger than in the past because she'd quit smoking on January 1 and began doing forty minutes of vocal calisthenics several hours before every concert. "I was smoking almost three packs a day," she said. "Kools. Menthols…I would absolutely do a commercial for that [nicotine] patch. The night before I quit, I smoked about 500 cigarettes and drank some hard liquor, which I never do anymore, because I knew it would make me feel extra bad." Now, if she gets a nicotine fit, she slaps on a seven-milligram patch, and says, "I just go with it."[5]

It was the solo tour Lindsey completed in 1992 that made it easier to see himself as part of Fleetwood Mac again. It had been crucial "not for perception in the public necessarily or record sales for [his album] *Out of the Cradle* but finding and putting together something that was *not* Fleetwood Mac and represented a broader range of possibilities.

"The whole tenure in Fleetwood Mac was difficult. It was complicated, to say the least. The last few years were the most difficult. Everyone was pretty much at their worst. What became important was reorienting myself and finally getting some closure on Stevie after having to be around her all those years, then putting something together with people I hadn't known, really, and seeing myself in a different light through their eyes. [It was] a very important year for my confidence and realizing there was a lot that could be done out there. [It] brought me to a point where I had a lot more to give when I was pulled back into the Fleetwood Mac thing."

On August 20, 1997, Fleetwood Mac released the live album, *The Dance*. It was the twentieth anniversary of their phenomenally successful *Rumours* album. The show and tour was a compilation from Fleetwood Mac's best hits with a few new songs such as Stevie's "Sweet Girl." Stevie also performed "Silver Springs" live and after so many years recorded it for the *The Dance* CD, video, and DVD. It was even released as a single.

The Mac was back and better than ever, though Stevie has admitted it was an emotional experience. "Every once in a while something will hit me, and I'll almost burst into tears. It doesn't happen too often. It happened once on the last Fleetwood Mac tour, at a certain part in 'Sweet Girl.' [singing] Go through the…traffic, it goes through the fog/The sun is burning me, and you come walking out in the rain with me—something like that. I just started thinking about how Christine [McVie] didn't want to go back out on the road, and it upset me. I was thinking of her as Sweet Girl! She was standing right there, next to me. I have to be careful because I'm real emotional and I could go that way every night if I let myself. I don't, because it's not going to do me any good to burst into tears in the middle of 'Silver Springs' or something. So I keep the emotion at a certain level."[6]

In an interview for *New York Post's* gossip column, Stevie, with candor, shared a little bit about her family dynamics. "My mom said to me, 'Stevie, you are so blessed. This time, since you guys aren't so screwed up, you can see the world again, and all the castles and the Sistine Chapel, which you never bothered to see before.' When we used to play Europe, we just slept all day. I never saw the Eiffel Tower. I never wanted to get up early."

The recording received many accolades, including a British Recognition Award and three Grammy nominations. *The Dance,* while nominated for Best Pop Album, was overshadowed by James Taylor's *Hour Glass.* "Silver Springs" was nominated for Best Pop Performance by a Group or Duo with Vocals but lost out to Jamiroquai's "Virtual Insanity." "The Chain" was nominated in the Best Rock Performance by a Group or Duo with Vocals but The Wallflowers went home with the award for "One Headlight."

On why Fleetwood Mac has continued to be successful, Stevie had this to say. "No matter how fabulous and big time Fleetwood Mac was, there was always a really dark edge to it. Fleetwood Mac was anything but a happy soft-rock band. There was a lot of darkness and a lot of dark stuff going on. And so maybe people relate to that darkness because they knew it wasn't easy for us and that we went through the drugs, criticism, the big success and the dropping down and going back up."[7]

When asked how he felt about the reunion, Lindsey, always thoughtful, honest, and open, told *Billboard* magazine, "But, you know, Stevie is in a really good place, and there was something good about it. You just have to keep watching yourself to make sure that you don't get petty. I went in and I tried to make nice, and it wasn't hard. It's sweet, it's nostalgic; you could cry over it if you let yourself."

"This was like the girl I used to live with again. And it was no longer bittersweet, like it had been for so long, it was just sweet."[8]

With all the years of pain, loss, and separation, Lindsey has grown quite introspective. He spoke with *Rolling Stone* about how things were different. "No matter what, some of that chemistry will always be there. It's just getting channeled into the performance without being so destructive or without being such a personal assault. For all of us, that 12 years I was in the band was kind of an exercise in emotional denial."

He went on to express his contentment. "We're taking it one step at a time. My shrink would say this is the best thing I've ever done. Take those emotional risks! Aside from any career strategy, it's just been a good, positive, healing interaction. If nothing else happens, this is a nice closure. That's enough."

In her interview with Aidan Smith of *Scotsman.com News*, Stevie expressed how nostalgic the reunion had been. "Before each show, as we gather outside our dressing rooms, Mick bends down from his lofty height and kisses me on the forehead and that's heavy. Then Lindsey and I, we climb into this little lift to be hoisted on to the stage, and he clasps his hands behind his back and I hold onto them, and for those 40 seconds we're united. It feels like we're in love again." She went on to explain how it felt without all the substances. "The truly incredible thing is we're realizing that you can perform a two-and-a-half hour gig without being high and still have a fantastic time. This will sound a bit pathetic to normal people but we feel kind of proud that we can do that without being the drug addict/alcoholics we used to be."

The Dance tour started in September and lasted until November. They played every major city in the United States but never made it to Canada, Europe, or Australia because the tour was cut short. Christine McVie, despite being persuaded otherwise, was ready to give up the rock 'n' roll touring lifestyle in favor of her English home life and solo career.

Stevie was asked whether Christine was the reason the tour ended before Europe. "That's exactly the way it was. About halfway through the tour, she just was not happy. And it was hard for everybody. What can you say? 'Get happy?' Been there, done that—that's how she feels. So we just had to let her go. [But] we're never gonna break this band up again, so without her, it won't ever go back together. In two years, Chris may be very bored. And you know Mick is hoping that Chris gets very bored!"9 Once again, Stevie displayed her definitive nature. She was right that the band wouldn't go on in its *Rumours* line-up, but the future did hold another Fleetwood Mac album and tour.

Rolling Stone, in its 1998 Q&A session, asked Stevie about her experience on *The Dance* tour: "You were so clearly the fan favorite during the tour. How does the rest of the band deal with that now?" Stevie gave her assessment and, not unlike when she wanted Lindsey's solo career to be more successful than hers, she was sensitive to his needs. "I think probably it's fine and fairly easy for everybody in the band except Lindsey. I think it's hard for Lindsey because we started out together. I think he goes, like, 'When did you do all this? Why do you get this kind of reaction?' And I think that is hard for him. So I don't talk to him a lot about it. It's kind of like, what we do together is what we talk about. I don't want to make Lindsey unhappy. I care about him and want him to be happy."

While Stevie does tend to be the center of Fleetwood Mac fan adulation, she remained more subdued during the *Say You Will* tour. It was as if she wanted to ensure Lindsey had top billing. Along with the other band members, she was inducted into the Rock and Roll Hall of Fame in January 1998.

Stevie—1990s
(© Photorazzi)

Stevie—1990s
(Photo by Willie Jennings)

Nine

Timespace and Street Angel

In 1991, having completed Fleetwood Mac's *Behind the Mask* album, Stevie released *Timespace: The Best of Stevie Nicks*. The album is a compilation of ten years of solo hits and a few new songs such as "Love's A Hard Game To Play," "Desert Angel" (a tribute to the Gulf War troops), and Jon Bon Jovi's "Sometimes It's A Bitch," which was also released as a single. She wrote personal notations on each song for the *Timespace* album. "I just felt like it was time. Finally after all these years, people have to understand why these songs were written and why I sometimes get so emotional on stage, why I sometimes burst into tears. It isn't because I'm a cornball, but there's a real reason. It's that I'm reliving an experience that happened to me and that I wrote about."[1] She went on tour to support the album with a stage set that included an English living room with high, starlit windows, burgundy velvet drapes, and Persian rugs.

Although her addiction to Klonopin continued to sap her energy and creative capabilities, Stevie entered the studio free from her commitments to Fleetwood Mac and started work on her fifth album, *Street Angel*. She worked with artists Sandy Stewart and Mike Campbell and also recorded Bob Dylan's "Just Like A Woman." Dylan even joined Stevie in the studio to record the guitar and harmonica parts for the song.

On how it felt to no longer be a part of Fleetwood Mac, Stevie didn't hold back when talking with Larry Katz from the *Boston Herald*. "It's really easier. This is the first time I'll go out by myself and I won't be carrying around a feeling of guilt. See, when I was in Fleetwood Mac, I'd know by the middle of one of my tours they were already getting mad at me. They'd be waiting for me like anxious cats. It takes the fun out of touring when other people don't think you should be doing it in the first place. Then when I got back, I'd have two days off and then I'd have to be in the studio, and the others would have already been in the studio for months. So they were never real happy to see me. So this is the first time I've ever gotten to completely concentrate on my show and put my whole heart in it. It's like when you get a divorce. You go on with your life and eventually realize you're free. It's an amazing feeling."

Street Angel reached gold status. The title song was not written in her typically autobiographical style. "It's a fictional story about a girl who is a homeless person who has been in the street, with her family, her whole life. They are just gypsies. Some rich guy falls in love with her and tries to lift her up by marrying her. She can't do it, 'cause she can't give up her other life in the street. It's not a political comment on how to save the homeless."[2] "Jane," the last song on the album, was inspired by renowned primatologist Jane Goodall.

This was Stevie's only solo album never certified platinum, a remarkable feat for any artist. Still, she was not happy. Her prolonged Klonopin addiction fostered deterioration in creativity. Her records were not selling as well, and she became more and more withdrawn. Isolated and depressed, Stevie ate for comfort. She was lethargic and soon had gained thirty pounds.

During the tour supporting her new album, the press focused on her size rather than her music. One review by Glen Kenney from the *Daily News* must have really hurt. "If there is any analogue to Sunset Boulevard's Norma Desmond, it must be Stevie Nicks. Imagine Stevie roaming through her mansion swaddled in frilly fabric, believing that the world outside is still held in thrall by the Maxfield Parrish-tinted visions of the glazed-eyed doe this middle-aged woman no longer is. Her latest album, *Street Angel*, is the aural equivalent to that clueless anachronistic script."

Just as she feared could happen based on the lyrics from her hit "After the Glitter Fades," Stevie was not herself. She didn't even like the record. "Klonopin literally sucked away my creativity and my soul. It was a terrible record, and when I got out of rehab I tried to fix it, but it was unfixable. You can't write beautiful songs and sing beautifully and be happy when you're on that type of drug. It turns you into a person who doesn't care about anything. You don't care about the music; you just go in and sing it. And that's what everybody heard when they listened to that record. They heard that I really didn't care." After a three-month tour, she "made the *Street Angel* album go away completely. I have never listened to it since."[3]

On how she felt about the fan and critical reaction, Stevie told *Entertainment Weekly*, "Horrified. With life in general. And I was really heavy, and I was so unhappy. I said, 'I'll never, ever go on stage weighing this much again ever, so I'm finished unless I lose weight.' And luckily, in the next three years, I did. But it took a long time. I was at the end of my contract with Atlantic, and I didn't have a new record deal, and I felt like 'Wow, I guess talent no longer matters. So, obviously, get another job or something!' I felt really bad. And I said, 'I'll never forget this feeling.'"

People magazine's review was right on target. "The songs on the album [*Street Angel*] are confessional in nature and love, loneliness and survival are recurring themes." *Rolling Stone's* Kara Manning also wrote a poignant review. "Although Stevie Nicks's child woman personality has served her 20 years, it's long overdue for the doe-eyed innocent to get tough…Refusing to spit and kick like Bonnie Raitt or Kim Gordon, she trembles instead, a little girl made helpless by uncaring men and her own isolation."

"I became the whatever person. Do you want to go out? Whatever. Do you want me to come over? I don't care. My writing became that. My songs became that. I gained 30 pounds. And the public noticed—they weren't nice. The criticism was very hard and very deserved, 'cause I was screwed up. Everyone was just being truthful."[4]

Late in 1994, Stevie finally recognized she had to do something. "The drug changed me from a tormented, productive artist to an indifferent woman," Nicks told *People* in 1998. She became so zonked-out and barely remembers her solo tour in 1989. "I vegetated into my own little world." While hosting a bridal shower for a friend in late 1993, Stevie fell into a fireplace, gashed her head but didn't feel a thing. Realizing she had to get off the Klonopin, Stevie checked in to the Exodus Drug Rehabilitation Center in Los Angeles. She was surprised at how difficult it was to beat her prescription drug habit. It was considerably worse than the cocaine experience. "It would have been so easy for me to call a limo from rehab, go to another hospital and ask for Demerol because I was in so much pain," Stevie continued. "Instead I stood on the edge of the cliff and said, 'I need to live.'"

When asked about the difference between getting off cocaine and Klonopin, Stevie spoke candidly. "[Getting off prescriptions drugs was worse], so much worse. I was in [rehab], sick for 45 days, really sick. I watched generations of drug addicts come in and go out. 'Good-bye!' 'Hi!' 'Bye!' You know, the heroin people: 12 days, 3 days of psychotherapy, and they're gone—and I'm still there. I want people, when somebody says 'I want to put you on Klonopin,' to run screaming from the room. In those 45 days [of rehab], my hair turned gray, my skin molted, I had a headache from the second I got in there until the day I left, I didn't sleep, and I couldn't go to any of the therapy things, I was so sick. It was awful."[5]

When released from the treatment center, Stevie headed home to Phoenix. For three years, she lived like a recluse, very much out of the public eye. "She was getting to know herself and getting to know Stevie again, Lori Perry Nicks, her sister-in-law, has said. "It's a long process of healing and there was nothing anybody could really do. She was very sad for a long time. Very unhappy. There was nothing that she could find in life that really mattered that much to her."[6]

Looking back on her life and her nearly two-decade drug addiction, she has decided to be open and give people a chance to avoid the pain she went through. "I want people to know, if they followed my career and wondered what happened between about 1988 and 1993, those years are just nearly gone for me. I had just stopped doing cocaine, and I was totally fine. But to soothe everybody's feathers around me, I went to a psychiatrist. Boy, I wish I'd gotten sick that day. He put me on Klonopin, like a Valium thing. By 1989, it wasn't that I didn't write well, I just stopped writing. And because of being on a tranquilizing drug, of course you make very bad decisions—I fired people, I hired people...It nearly destroyed me. I think the real reason why I'm angry is, I was successful, I was doing well in a man's world, I'm a rock star—I didn't have anything to be depressed about!"[7]

It was Tom Petty who helped Stevie come out of her writer's funk. She asked for his help writing a song. He told her she could do it herself for God's sake and to get back to it! "It was over dinner at the Ritz Carlton in Phoenix, in Paradise Valley, and The Heartbreakers were there to play," she told *In News Weekly* while promoting *Trouble in Shangri-La*. "The night before I went down and had dinner with him and he gave me one of the most quintessential lectures of my life where he basically made me very aware that 'I know you've had a hard time but get over it. Songwriting is what you do, Stevie, the last thing in the world you should do is ask me to write a song for you because that's what you DO.' And it took someone like him to really say that to me for me to listen, because if anybody else had said that to me I probably would have just walked out."

Returning the favor, Stevie spoke with Sarah McLachlan in 1995, offering advice and friendship to a fellow musician. The conversation was recorded for *Interview* magazine. "You can always call me. I have been through just about every possible thing that you could go through, and I've just given up everything you could possibly give up for this. And I wonder sometimes if I made the right decisions. There are a lot of things that I would love to tell you that might make a difficult time a little easier for you. I'll give you my phone number so that you can call me when you're in the middle of Toronto, bummed out, and I can tell you that everything's gonna be all right."

Everything was all right. In 1996, Stevie recorded a duet with Lindsey Buckingham for the movie *Twister*. The song "Twisted" was their first musical collaboration since Lindsey left Fleetwood Mac in 1987. It was the fresh start they needed to mend their broken relationship. Soon after in 1997, Stevie found herself right back in the band she loved, performing classic songs on *The Dance* tour with the best Fleetwood Mac line-up ever.

Stevie with her dad, signing autographs after "A Christmas Carol," Dec. 20, 1996
(Photo by Debbi Radford)

Stevie smiling at her fans after "A Christmas Carol," Dec. 20, 1996
(Photo by Melissa Loukas)

Ten

Enchanted and *Trouble in Shangri-La*

Once the Fleetwood Mac reunion tour had finished, Stevie found herself with time to dedicate to her solo career once again. This time it was a compilation of her best songs. She released, *Enchanted: The Works of Stevie Nicks*, a three-CD box set, in 1998. For Stevie, it was like a photo album. Her songs are all written about something that happened in her life, so there are memories and associated experiences that go along with each of them. Rolling Stone's review by Rob Sheffield was gratifying. "Stevie Nicks is more than a rock icon: She's the high priestess of her own religion, ruling a world of prancing gypsies, gold-dust princesses and white-winged doves, all without going anywhere with a sensible shoe. Like David Bowie or Bryan Ferry, Nicks has spent a career turning her private fantasies into an elaborate pop mythology. And even when she gets carried away, she still has that soulful ache in her voice. On "Enchanted," a three-CD retrospective of her solo career, you can hear how faithfully Nicks has followed her vision. As she confesses in 1983's excellent "Nightbird," "I wear boots all summer long."

"Enchanted" combines live rarities and B sides with radio hits like "Stand Back." But the emotional highlight is "Ooh My Love" (originally buried in the long-forgotten "The Other Side of the Mirror"), about a princess who feels like a prisoner in her own castle even though she's still terrified of the world outside. It's Nicks' love letter to her fans, and, like the rest of "Enchanted," it makes you admire her fierce compassion for the lost girls in her flock. She's lasted so long as an icon because she's never forgotten how it feels to teeter in high heels on the edge of seventeen." About a year after the release, the box set was certificated gold in the United States, a significant accomplishment for a three-CD set. The *Enchanted* tour in the summer of 1998 was the largest Stevie had ever done. It was designed to support her passion for eradicating heart disease. Twenty five cents from each ticket sold to the 42 shows went toward supporting Arizona Heart Foundation's Heart Healthy Lessons for Children program and other areas of research and education. The concert at the Woodstock festival closed the tour in early August.

Prior to the start of the tour, Stevie appeared on the *David Letterman Show*. As he introduced her for her performance, he called her his ex-wife and later asked if he could tour with her and meet her at her hotel after the shows! Stevie managed to perform, seemingly unaffected, but he reminded her of his quip when she sat next to him afterward for the traditional interview. She sheepishly put her hands over her face, showing her embarrassment but kept up the charade and said she guessed it would be okay since after all they'd been married! Stevie really is quite shy and admittedly is uncomfortable when speaking in front of an audience. She also performed on *The Tonight Show with Jay Leno*, though Jay had no such surprises in store.

The year 1998 was a busy year and full of accolades and disclosure for Stevie. She was a subject for *VH1: Behind the Music* and later filmed her *VH1: Storytellers* episode, a show where she sang her classics and described the evolution of her songs. In addition, she was ranked fourteenth on *VH1: 100 Greatest Women of Rock & Roll*, and *Rolling Stone* crowned her the "Reigning Queen of Rock & Roll." She was even named one of the "50 Most Beautiful People in the World" by *People* magazine.

Later that year Stevie worked with Sheryl Crow on two songs for the *Practical Magic* soundtrack, a remake of the Buckingham Nicks and Fleetwood Mac song *"Crystal"* and *"If You Ever Did Believe."* The latter was also released as a single.

The year was not without additional unwanted notoriety, according to *Capitol Hill Blue.* "In July, while a religious organization ran a controversial national advertising campaign offering help to gays to "change" into heterosexuals, Ronald Anacelteo, thirty-eight, was ordered by a court in Los Angeles to stay away from singer Stevie Nicks, whom Anacelteo thought could change him from gay to straight. According to a law enforcement officer, Anacelteo (who is not affiliated with the ad campaign) "is a self-proclaimed homosexual" who believes that Nicks can "heal" his homosexuality and "find [him] a woman to marry." *E! Online* reported that he planned to abduct Stevie from her Denver performance and absorb her supposed spiritual powers. She obtained a restraining order against him.

Her impact on gay culture is significant, highlighted by the annual *Night of a Thousand Stevies* drag extravaganza in Manhattan. "The fact that anybody cares enough about my music and my chiffon to gather and have a party in my honor, that's just an incredible thing."[1] In addition, gay filmmaker Todd Stephens (who wrote 1998s gay coming of age tale *Edge of Seventeen,* a title inspired by Nicks's rock classic) released the fictional film *Gypsy83* starring Sara Rue as a Stevie-obsessed fan, road-tripping her way to the party.

Other notoriety in 1998 included Lucy Lawless's parody of Stevie on *Saturday Night Live* in a skit called "Stevie Nicks's Fajita Round-Up." In the spoof, Nicks runs a Tex-Mex cantina in Arizona, where all her signature dishes are take-offs on her song titles, and her food choices are tied to her drug addictions. Lucy began the skit with "Hello, I'm Stevie Nicks. Do you like the music of my band, Fleetwood Mac? And do you like fajitas, flautas, quesadillas, and other Tex-Mex specialties? Then come on down to my new restaurant in Sedona, Arizona-Stevie Nicks's Fajita Roundup. In the seventies, I dedicated myself to witchcraft, Lindsey Buckingham, and cocaine. But now I use that same energy and dedication to bring you an affordable dining experience you'll never forget." In one episode of *South Park,* she was mistaken for a goat when she and Fleetwood Mac performed in Afghanistan for U.S. soldiers. Stevie was also the basis for the character "Jynx" on the popular children's TV series *Pokémon.*

Another 1998 milestone was Stevie's fiftieth birthday. "For me a 50th birthday is an excuse for people to buy you fabulous presents. I got a diamond pendant and a diamond ring. There was no reason not to have a great birthday."[2] And at 50 and crowd favorite during the highly successful Dance tour, she felt like the old Stevie Nicks again. "And that," according to Sheryl Crow, "is a combination of beauty, mystery, talent and power."

The Nicks family made headlines in *Allstar News* on June 3, 1999. "Former Fleetwood Mac singer Stevie Nicks and her family were being sued for allegedly lending credibility to a woman accused of bilking investors in a no-kill animal shelter. Britney Marx, thirty-four, faced charges of defrauding someone of nearly $400,000 by purporting to build the animal shelter, then spending the money on herself. Stevie, her brother, and her mother were accused in the lawsuit of assisting Ms. Marx by staying silent about her previous fraud convictions and endorsing the shelter. The lawsuit was filed by Dale R. Lumb, one of the people Ms. Marx borrowed money from. 'God knows we had no idea she borrowed any money,' said Barbara Nicks, the singer's mother. 'It just kills me to think she borrowed money from people and didn't pay it back.'"

Stevie also spent some time finishing something she'd started many years earlier. Interrupted while working on a solo project in 1997 when the Fleetwood Mac reunion album and tour became a reality, she finally had a chance to return to the studio to wrap *Trouble in Shangri-La.* Released in 2001, it would be her first album with all new material since 1994s *Street Angel.* "When I tell people this record took seven years, it didn't really take seven years. It just took that much time for it all to be done. If I really went back and went through my journals and really logged the actual time, I would say this record probably took about seven months."[3]

In the studio, Stevie still had significantly less confidence than earlier in her career and remained humiliated by her behavior during the drugging days. During the infamous dinner in Phoenix with Tom Petty to discuss his possible participation on the record, a pivotal event occurred. "I was horrified about things I did to people during eight years of Klonopin and Prozac. I almost couldn't get over it. Tom recognized that. He said, 'I know you're upset, but you didn't go looking for those drugs on the street. Nobody's mad at you anymore. Everyone is over it except you.' It snapped my brain." Petty rejected her invitation and told her, "You didn't have babies because you wanted to write songs, so go home and create more babies." Stevie explained, "I went straight to my living room and started to write. That dinner at the Ritz-Carlton was worth a jillion dollars."[4]

Stevie felt the time was right for releasing *Trouble in Shangri-La*. "I'm very, very proud of this work, and I would've not put this record out until I knew it was really done and that I really felt it was really good," she said. "I would've worked on it for another 10 years if it hadn't've actually kind of almost finished itself in the last couple of months. It just went, like, 'I'm finished. I'm done.'"[5]

Stevie collaborated with Sheryl Crow, who co-produced five tracks. "Sheryl's very organized," she admitted in an online chat with *Entertainment Weekly*. "You have to be. You can't be la-la-la-la like me and be a really good producer." "I guess my role in this [producing *Trouble in Shangri-La*] is really to try and create what she feels is an accurate picture of who she is," Sheryl told *Reuters*. "She's a really prolific writer. I think the thing she has suffered in the last few years is when she goes into the studio, there's always a male producer that wants to make her into something that is maybe not as intimate as what she sees her music as being. Trying to get that on tape is going to be the real trick."

Through it all they developed a deep personal friendship. "First, Sheryl's brilliant, she's an amazing songwriter, singer and musician," Stevie told *Billboard* magazine. "But she's also someone who gets it. She understands the life of a woman in rock 'n' roll. There's no room for playing games with her or saying, 'You don't understand what I'm going through.' She understands, and that's brought us closer than I can explain."

Stevie continued by discussing their collaboration on "Sorcerer." "Sheryl challenged me to explore different areas of my voice. It was fun to do, and it wound up working so well within the song's arrangement."

Stevie felt that singing with Sheryl was similar to singing with Lindsey, given her talent for duets.

"She and I have had such a similar path," Sheryl told the *Boston Globe.* "She became well-known at 29 and I got my first record deal when I was 29. We're also similar in that we're both matriarchal. When we go out on the road, we take care of everybody. We're not just the captain of the ship, we are the mother—and the person who is challenging everyone musically. But when you come home, it's a different thing. That was my experience when I came off the road this last time. All of a sudden, the family that I built around me wasn't my family. They all went home to their families. And that's what motivates you to continue to go out on the road."

According to the *Miami Herald,* Crow was honored to work with Stevie. "To even be in the same room as Stevie was a dream come true for me. To work with her was beyond description. It was extraordinary." Sheryl has described Stevie as the kind of person you feel like you've known all your life.

On Stevie's request, Sheryl wrote and produced "It's Only Love" for the album. She also played guitar and provided background vocals. She serves as a confidante for Stevie and captured the trade-off in her life between love and her ride in rock 'n' roll.

Macy Gray provided backup vocals for "Bombay Sapphire." "The only reason Macy [Gray] is on the record is because we're managed by the same people. Originally I wanted Sting to sing that little high part on 'Bombay Sapphire,' but I chickened out on calling him and I asked Macy to do it."[6]

"Her [Macy Gray] vibe is so wild, so intense," Stevie released in her press kit for the album. "She walks into the room and it's like everything starts to move. She's like a walking tornado. She's a total blast. We had a great time working on the song. Our voices blended so well together."

"My personal favorite [song on the TISL album] is 'Bombay Sapphire,'" Stevie told *VH1.com.* "When it says, 'I can see past you to the white sand,' that sentence right there is the whole reason for 'Bombay Sapphire.' It means that I'm really trying to get over something, and though I'm freaked out about it I'm looking to the green ocean and can see past all of these problems to the incredibly beautiful white sand and the ocean beyond it. I'm gonna be OK because I am movin' past you.

"And when 'Bombay Sapphire' almost got pulled off the record because it wasn't recorded right, I was horrified that one line was not gonna be on the record. It's really important for me to tell people that if they're in an unhappy situation they should not stay forever and be miserable." She discussed the song further for *Borders.com*. "Yes ['Bombay Sapphire' is my favorite on the album], because it is a song that I thought had a great message. I wrote it in Hawaii two years ago. At that point, in order to write the rest of the songs for this record, I really had to leave my *Enchanted* box set and Fleetwood Mac behind. Hawaii was very different than any place I'd ever been. Very green—jade green—very calm, very Zen. And I realized that if you take yourself to a great environment, you can just about get over anything.

"I was looking outside one day and it was like I was almost seeing my past as a little bit of something that I really wanted to leave behind for a while. I was looking past the past, out to the ocean and how beautiful it was and how white and inviting the sand was. I thought, I can see past you to the white sand and a message back to me that you are moving on now, you really are moving on. You are letting go of all that stuff that bothered you and you are moving forward. So, for me, it was very important that that song be on the record. I recorded that song two other times, and I didn't like it either time. I went back in for a third time and played it myself to get it the way I had written it when I was in Hawaii that night." It would seem the reunion tour with Lindsey opened some unresolved memories of pain and loss. Separation must have been quite difficult.

Stevie also produced "Bombay Sapphire" herself. "It was easy, because it was exactly what I wanted to do. It was done in one night. I really did have a vision for that song, and [on earlier attempts to record it] nobody else saw my vision. The first time it was too R&B, the second time it was too Wagner, dirge-like. The third time it was back to its little funky reggae self."[7] She even played keyboards on both "Bombay Sapphire" and "Planets of the Universe."

Sarah McLachlan played the piano and guitar while providing backup vocals on "Love Is," the song that Stevie wrote after her infamous dinner with Tom Petty. She also wrote "That Made Me Stronger" about the fortuitous advice she received over dinner about her songwriting. Steve Booker and Sandy Stewart wrote "Too Far From Texas" and Natalie Maines of the Dixie Chicks sang background vocals on the track.

In an interview with *Border.com* about her new album, Stevie told Maggie Bruber, "Well, several of the songs are about my relationship with Lindsey because I've just had magnificent things to write about. My life is incredible. It is exciting. I'm not married, I don't have children. I'm very free. I travel. I do stuff. I love my life. But Lindsey and I have come through this whole thing, and we are still friends somehow. He lives 10 minutes from me. I can jump in the car and go over there. He knows these songs are about him. He's been hearing these songs since they were written.

"I wrote 'Candlebright' before Lindsey and I left San Francisco. That was one of the songs we came here with to get our record deal for Buckingham Nicks. 'Candlebright' isn't really written about Lindsey, it's written about Lindsey and me, both of us. 'Planets of the Universe' is written about when Lindsey and I really broke up after the *Rumours* record. 'Sorcerer' is written about Lindsey and I coming to Hollywood from San Francisco. Lindsey had lived at home. He moved out of his parents' house, in with me, in Los Angeles. So those songs are about us. He knows that. He looked at me the other day and said, 'A lot of these songs are about me.' And I said, 'Aren't you just so flattered that you've been such an inspiration to me my whole life?' And you know what? He is flattered. But there's nothing in those songs that you can't know, because if there were, it wouldn't be in the song. I write from a specific experience and make it as general as I can so it will be able to reach out and be understood by a lot of people."

When Maggie suggested that "Shangri-La" might also describe Fleetwood Mac, Stevie explained, "Well, that's very interesting that you would say that because, even though I didn't set down to write any of it about Fleetwood Mac; in fact, some of the verses actually did touch on Fleetwood Mac. The first verse is absolutely about Lindsey and me. When I was writing it I really wasn't conscious of that because I just write long poems. I write poems with about 20 stanzas and then some of them have to go when you actually put it to a song. But 'I remember him, he was very young/No one spoke like him, he was someone/And I carried on, like I couldn't stop/All of it for us baby.' All of it for love basically. That verse is about him and that is how the verses started out. The rest of the verses are all about separate people. But they'd all come down to a very common thing, trouble in Shangri-La. 'You will never love again the way you love me,' the chorus to 'Planets of the Universe,' is reminiscent of Fleetwood Mac's 'The Chain.' 'The Chain' was my song. It was my words and my song put together with an instrumental Fleetwood Mac had going that had some of the same chords in it. Lindsey had heard me play the song on my guitar before and asked me, 'Could we use this, because that song will fit into this song?' Of course I said, 'Cool.'"

"Planets of the Universe" was written in 1976 when she was breaking up with Lindsey. Her lyrics, "Now I know, Well, I was wrong, To live for a dream, If I had my life to live over, I would never dream, no I still wish you gone, And I will live alone, Yes, I will live alone" clearly depict her feelings at the time. "That was a huge statement for me to make, a very harsh thing for me to say. It was just for six months [that I felt that]. I was depressed about love. The song was written when we were recording *Rumours* in San Francisco. I was tired of the city and very, very angry at Lindsey. How strange and funny, though, that I have lived alone all that time since."[8]

Maybe it's not so strange after all. Consider the evidence of several songs on the new album. In "Love Changes," she cut a man loose as soon as her passion wanes. In "Too Far from Texas," she has an affair with an unavailable married man. In "Candlebright," she's a nomad who can't be pinned down by love. "I don't like staying in one place long," she went on to say. "It's the way I'm happy. I live in two houses, in L.A. and Phoenix. When I get tired of one, I move on."

"Every Day," the Buddy Holly-like tune provided by esteemed song-writer and producer, John Shanks for their variety show appearances, featured Sheryl Crow's harmony and guitar. "Sorcerer," originally written in 1974, is a favorite of backup singer Sharon Celani. When asked what the song is about, Stevie had this to tell Maggie Bruber. "Well, 'Sorcerer' was written right after Lindsey and I had taken the *Buckingham Nicks* [album] cover in Hollywood. We had been living there for three years and it was really about how kind of scary Hollywood was, because we had just moved from San Francisco. We were fairly prim and had lived at home—Lindsey never lived out of the house, he moved from Mom and Dad's house to Los Angeles with me! So we were these like really fresh kids from San Francisco and Hollywood was heavy. We went to go do that photograph and there were models everywhere and I was walking around proclaiming to everyone I was a songwriter and not a model! [laughs] Because I knew, I just knew that I better make sure I push the songwriting and not the sex symbol thing because that will fade and the songwriting will stay, hopefully."

"Fall from Grace" is the rock 'n' roll linchpin on the album. Shanks felt the original version of the song had too many verses. It broke Stevie's heart. She doesn't like to let any of her words slip away. One session when Sheryl's friends, Laura Dern and Rosanna Arquette, were hanging out in the studio, they caught a glimpse of the original draft of the song. They all ganged up on John and won the war. Everything from the original draft made it to disc. Stevie describes the song as the perfect balance to "Edge of Seventeen" in terms of its energy level and penchant for becoming an onstage rock-out session.

Lindsey Buckingham, notoriously non-committal when it comes to Stevie's solo work, has said *Trouble in Shangri-La* is the best album she's ever released, thus giving her the approval she didn't think she would ever receive from the one she loves the most. He even played on "I Miss You," a beautiful song written about him. "Love Changes" was written about Lindsey as well. According to Stevie, the songs were written either before or after her long addiction to the prescription drug Klonopin. "When you're on that drug, you don't want to do anything." The clarity of her lyrics is also reflected in Nicks's choice to write in the first person rather than the third, her old preference. "It's riskier [to use the first person]," she said. "Then you're saying, 'This really is me.'"9

In preparation for her *Trouble in Shangri-La* tour, Stevie appeared with Sheryl Crow on both *Letterman* and *Leno*. Her tour ultimately grossed more than $13.3 million, according to *Billboard Boxscore* and was attended by nearly 300,000 fans.

In 2002, Stevie was nominated for a Grammy Award for Best Female Rock Vocal Performance for "Planets of the Universe" and was ranked number fifty-two on *VH1's 100 Sexiest Artists*. While promoting the album, Stevie was a guest on *The Rosie O'Donnell Show* and ran into the members of Destiny's Child, who were down the hall rehearsing for their weekend appearance on *Saturday Night Live*. They are big Stevie Nicks fans. In fact, the group's single, "Bootylicious," prominently features a guitar riff from "Edge of Seventeen." Indeed, Stevie was asked to appear in the "Bootylicious" video. She agreed, and it was shot in Los Angeles in May of 2001.

Stevie—Enchanted Tour in Manassas, VA, June 24, 1998
(Photo by Maryellen Suter)

Stevie—Enchanted Tour
Radio City Music Hall, 1998
(Photo by Ray Sette)

Stevie—Enchanted Tour, Woodstock August 14, 1998
(Photo by Kathy Uhlenbrock)

Stevie performing in 2001
(Photo by Barry Brecheisen)

Stevie, Lindsey, and Mick with the Clintons—January 6, 2001
(© *Barbara Kinney / CORBIS*)

Stevie with Sheryl Crow—
Blockbuster Entertainment
Awards, Shrine Auditorium,
Los Angeles, CA, April 10, 2001
(B. King / WireImage)

Stevie—Radio Music Awards,
Las Vegas, NV, October 26, 2001
(Trapper Frank / CORBIS)

Stevie with Cher (as Elvis) *VH1* Divas Las Vegas,
MGM Grand Arena, May 23, 2002
(Mazur / WireImage)

Eleven

Say You Will

In early 2001, Mick Fleetwood promised another Fleetwood Mac reunion some time in the near future. He believed that once Stevie and Lindsey had finished their respective solo projects, they would honor their commitment to doing another studio album and tour. The disappointment to most Fleetwood Mac fans, however, would be that the album and tour would not include beloved singer and keyboardist, Christine McVie. She was already working on her solo album and enjoying life in England.

In 2001 when Stevie released *Trouble In Shangri-La*, her first solo album in seven years, she told *Launch* that Mick's comments weren't just wishful thinking. "Mick and I are gonna make this happen. We're the strong ones, and we're gonna push this through if it kills us," she said. "We really want to do another record. Christine doesn't want to do it—she doesn't—and bless her heart, if that's what she wants, then that's what she's gonna get. She moved back to England. She wants to be an Englishwoman living in England, and you cannot make people do stuff."

As Lindsey Buckingham was readying the release of what would have been his fourth solo album, *Gift of Screws*, he went into the studio instead with Fleetwood Mac. His songs, along with Stevie's, now appear on 2003s *Say You Will*. "Yes, there seems to be a pattern there, doesn't it? This kind of intervention thing," Lindsey said in an interview with the *Rocky Mountain News*.

VH1 captured hours of the band's studio time in their rented Los Angeles home during the taping of *Destiny Rules*, a documentary on the making of *Say You Will*. Viewers have found the airing of the documentary, also available on DVD, a cathartic experience. The honesty, mutual respect, warmth, and love shone through despite typical challenges faced when making a record with four very different and creative musicians—particularly *these* four musicians.

"It's not easy for us. It never will be. It hasn't ever been. Whenever we get back into a room together and start working, we don't agree on a lot of stuff. Especially now, because we're really settled in our ways. It's no different than it was in 1975 when we went into rehearsal for Fleetwood Mac. We were fighting then, and we have fought all through every single record we have ever made. So I think if it wasn't like that, we'd probably all be walking around going, 'What's the matter with us?'" Lindsey added simply, "Our real lives have been laid bare in vinyl."[1]

Fleetwood Mac was no longer the biggest soap opera in rock 'n' roll; it was now a collection of four people doing what they love best and doing it with people who understood them better than anyone. However, Mick Fleetwood did remember several tense moments. "During the making of *Say You Will* I remember Lindsey one day turned around to Stevie and said, 'I've been looking at some of the words on this song, and if you cut some of these words out, I think the melody would work better,' And vroom! Stevie said, 'I'm not changing my words!' because she's a poet, and that's that."[2]

"I'd be totally lying if I said that record is what I wanted, because it isn't," she told *The Age* in Australia. "I argued with Lindsey all the way through it, and he argued with me. It wasn't very much fun, and I wasn't that pleased with the music. I felt my demos were better, which of course is easy to say, but I did. And what can I say? It wasn't a lot of fun." Despite the challenges, their onstage presence was quite warm. "We are extremely professional, and when we get up there on the stage we get lost on the fun parts of the show," she explained. "So it's never going to show anything bad, because we're always going to rise above and concentrate on the good things."

Lindsey and Stevie even fought and argued after the recording project. "There were some problems with the track-listing near the end," confided Lindsey. "Stevie was in Hawaii on vacation while I was in Los Angeles trying to master the album, and we got into some over-the-phone conflicts. It's been hard for Stevie to feel good about what we've accomplished, and I really hope she will at some point." Close to tears, he continued. "She's yet to say 'Good work on my songs, Lindsey.'"[3]

Stevie incredulously addressed his concern in her interview with the *Mirror* with whom Lindsey had stated something similar. "Did he say that to you? My God. All I can say is he worked his butt off. I give him all the credit. He took my little skeleton songs and turned them into fully finished pieces. The way we work hasn't changed and he is an immense talent, a craftsman beyond belief. I knew that the first time we met."

While the soap opera does seem to be over, Stevie continues to write a number of her songs about her former lover, Lindsey Buckingham. When asked whether people still tend to assume that Stevie and Lindsey's lyrics are about each other, he was quite forthcoming. "Yeah, they probably do," he laughs. "And in Stevie's case, at least some of them may be. Why 'may be?' Because it's not for me to say if they're about me. I suspect some of them are, but then Stevie has written songs all through our relationship that I assumed were about me, and then discovered that they weren't, or that they were hybrids. I can be as confused about that as the general listener."[4]

"'Thrown Down' is about Lindsey," Nicks admitted, "but I wrote that around the time of *The Dance* tour in 1997. Let's just say he continues to be a well of inspiration, which is terrific."[5]

Stevie described the meaning of her title cut, "Say You Will" for *Performing Songwriter*. "Everybody's experienced it—when you like somebody, it makes you a different person. It changes you and it changes you in a minute. But that song is not just about Lindsey. It's about a movie I saw about Arturo Sandoval, the trumpet player. I loved this movie, and I just loved the way that through all the pain and separation, they managed to do music and stay happy and keep love alive, and dancing and rhythm and music, how healing it was. That was really my inspiration for that song."

Stevie, never without confidence when it comes to her songwriting, continued. "You have this great chorus that basically says, 'If you dance with me, you won't be mad at me anymore. We can be in a huge argument, but if we put on some music and start to dance, everything will be great.' Then I had to think about what to make the verses about. So I went back over all my relationships with people and think of different ways that I have felt when I wanted basically to burst into song and sing that chorus. Give me one more chance. That's what came out of it. It's funny because, we just did an interview the day before yesterday, and I don't think any of the band knows that that was the reason I wrote the song."

Stevie remains single and a very busy woman. When asked about her relationship with Lindsey, Stevie, in 1997, exclaimed in her trademark assuredness, "I was as close to being married as I ever will be again." When listening to her lyrics on songs like "Destiny Rules" and "Thrown Down," it's difficult to know whether she is still in love with Lindsey or merely exploiting the most notorious publicly displayed musical soap opera ever.

Most likely, it's a little of both. Stevie is a master at understanding what her audience wants from her, and she will always love Lindsey on some level. "Things for Lindsey and I are never going to be mellow—never have been, never will be...[but] there are enough things now that we agree on that it's possible for us to work together again. When people say, 'Gee, great rage leads to great art,' a certain part of that really is true. The tragedy of our relationship makes it very interesting to watch."[6]

When asked if she and Lindsey are now able to discuss their relationship more openly, Stevie offered an honest answer. "You want the truth? We don't talk a lot about our past. We never have. It's like 'Do we need to go there?' And it hasn't turned out so bad, has it? Each of us has good, balanced lives now, and we're still able to make music together. So apart from being married and having our own family, what more could Lindsey and I have asked for?"

"Ilume," one of Stevie's songs on the *Say You Will* album, was written about the September 11 tragedy. She was in New York when the World

Trade Center was attacked, and "Ilume" portrays her feelings at the time. "My Rochester show was cancelled because of an act of war, and at one point we had a military escort on our wing. That whole period nearly drove me into a mental home."[7]

Mick Fleetwood read Stevie's poetry before she came in with the music. "She was very unsettled by 9/11, as we all were. The groove for "Illume" is incredibly simple, and she was like: 'Is this any good? Is it doing enough?' I said, 'In my opinion, Stevie, this is all about you; this is your modern-day "Gold Dust Woman." It has that Edith Piaf element coming through; that thing where the singer's relationship with the lyric is incredibly personal and powerful.' "[8]

"Running Through the Garden," while seemingly describing Stevie's tumultuous life, was actually written about someone else's trials. She explained her inspiration for *Performing Songwriter* in 2003. "I wrote that song around 1985. It's about the story "Rapaccini's Daughter" by Nathaniel Hawthorne. We didn't realize it until it was completely recorded. I thought it was a Twilight Zone episode I'd seen on TV fifteen or twenty years ago. But it's the story of this girl who's raised in this beautiful Italian villa and her dad is this gardener and he raised all these poisonous plants and he like infused the poisons into her. It's very hazy what I remember about the story. She became poisonous, so if anybody were to kiss her, they would die. And she could never leave, because she's addicted to the poison. So everybody's like, 'Wow, that's an incredible story.' There's a picture that Christine did, a drawing, and Chris is an incredible artist, probably twenty years ago, and she gave it to me, and it's her, it's the girl in the song. So I went back and forth about maybe calling it "Rapaccini's Daughter," but I thought I'd have to get publishing rights and all that, so I left it "Running Through The Garden."

"Silver Girl," a song some may have perceived purely autobiographical, was actually inspired by Sheryl Crow. "The first couple of lines are definitely about Sheryl," Stevie explained. "And when I thought about writing a whole song to this poem I had called "Silver Girl," I thought, 'Well, this whole song could be about Sheryl and also about all the rock and roll women, be they Norah Jones, Avril Lavigne, Michelle Branch, Stevie Nicks,

Gwen Stefani, whoever. That song is about the great parts, and also the difficulties, of being rock-star women."9

One of the songs that created great controversy between the artists was Lindsey's "Come." Stevie felt the song was too provocative and didn't want it in the set mix for the tour. ("Think of me, sweet darlin'/Every time you don't come".) It has been alleged that Lindsey wrote the lyric about Anne Heche, a former girlfriend who later had a lesbian relationship with Ellen DeGeneres. "That surprised me as much as it did everybody else," Buckingham told *Independent Review*.

Another contention was Stevie's clothes for the tour, Stevie admitted when asked why she had changed her style. "Mr. Buckingham is never crazy about my flamboyant clothes and I've just come off one hundred and thirty-five shows where his comment to me was like 'Can't you just be a little more casual?' So I said, 'Ok' and I went into a little black sweater that comes up to here with little pearl buttons and I did exactly what he wanted...I became way more casual for the Fleetwood Mac shows and, you know, it was great, it was fine and actually it was a very fabulous outfit...it was a little more sedate but it was still fabulous."10

During the *Say You Will* tour, Lindsey's niece, Cory Buckingham, traveled with the band and published tour diaries on the Internet. Several of her accounts revealed the lighter side of touring. "Stevie's manager has a little dog; I think he's a Maltese. A little white, soft and cuddly, energetic dog. He's a total doll, and he's friends with Stevie's two Yorkies. Anyway, he has a new trick. Stevie's manager holds a treat up in the air and says 'Standback! Stand Back' and moves her hand around in a circle, and he stands up on his hind legs and twirls just like Stevie does. It is so damn cute you just want to eat him. Stevie got a huge kick out of that one."

Cory also captured what its like to travel with Stevie. "There were only a few of us left in the building; most of the crew had gone back to the hotel for the night. (To enjoy this anecdote you'll need to know that we all carry radios at the gigs to communicate.) So I'm standing outside on the loading dock when someone starts singing over the radio. It seems Stevie was bored, so she took Karen's radio [Stevie's manager] and decided to indulge our Production Assistant by giving an impromptu performance of

"Illume," our PA's favorite Stevie song. After her radio debut, I asked if she was taking requests, and she was...so I got a radio performance of "Storms," from *Tusk*. I can't say how many of the little things I'll really remember when this tour is over, but that will certainly be one of them, it was very sweet."

It was important to Stevie to capture the tour in progress. "Stevie has been going crazy with her camera. She has this little digital camera that she takes everywhere. The best part...and I say this with love...is that she doesn't really know how to use it. Every time she takes a picture, she has to take it three times while saying 'this damn camera.' It's a riot. She takes pictures of everything and always says we will remember this tour."

It's clear how much Cory loves Stevie. "Personally the second show in Sydney was the most memorable for me, but only because I got in a bit of trouble. The trouble only lasted about the length of one song before it was cleared up...but it was the longest song of my life. To make a long story very short, there was a misunderstanding as to what song was supposed to come after 'Peacekeeper,' and in front of 10,000 people Ms. Stevie Nicks pointed to me and blamed me for this little screw up, she also called me by my full name, which as we all know from having mothers, that this always means you're in trouble. After 'Say You Will,' when Stevie went stage right to get her 'Rhiannon' top, Karen cleared up the misunderstanding and was sent to give me Stevie's apology, which was sweet. I met Stevie in the quick change tent after Rhiannon to give her a hard time about it, and as soon as she saw me she just covered her face and smiled, gave me a hug and apologized, it was really funny. After the show the crew definitely gave me a hard time about it. The next show during 'Second Hand News' she came over to my side of the stage, looked down at me, smiled and gave her tambourine a little shake in my direction, she's very funny."

As one of the matriarchs of rock 'n' roll, Stevie believes she has earned the right to be quite outspoken about the antics of younger entertainers. She was appalled by Madonna's publicity stunt kiss with Britney Spears at the *MTV* Awards. "I thought it was the most obnoxious moment in television history. Madonna will be fine. Madonna is Madonna. She does what she wants. She will get over this. But will Britney get over it? I don't know.

First of all, Madonna is too old to be kissing someone who is 22," the Fleetwood Mac singer told Nui Te Koha from the *Herald Sun*. "And Britney should be smarter than that. Hopefully, she will figure a way out of this hole she has dug for herself.

"Spears and Christina Aguilera should wear more clothes and try writing decent songs. I personally have never been to a strip club, but I turn on *MTV* and see in every single video what it must be like to be at a strip club. I think the mystery is gone, and if you have no mystery, then you aren't even sexy. Real sexuality and sensuality is in the music, and all these girls, vis-à-vis, Britney Spears, Christina Aguilera and on and on, should go back to writing songs and start over because it won't last and they won't last. When they are 55, they won't be around and that's sad because I think a lot of those girls are very talented. But they are signing their own death warrants." Koha also reported Nicks as saying, "Madonna, who I'm guessing orchestrated the whole thing, attempted to get Jennifer Lopez, AKA J.Lo, to join in the on stage kissing session. J.Lo basically told Madonna to kiss off."

Stevie with Lindsey Buckingham, *Say You Will* Tour,
Camden, NJ—September 12, 2004
(Photo by Tiffany Sledzianowski)

Twelve

Stevie Does Vegas and Tours with Don Henley

In May of 2005, Stevie Nicks was larger than life on the marquis at Caesar's Palace in Las Vegas. She performed four shows in the Colosseum, giving Celine Dion a break from her nightly show. She also ended her 2005 summer tour on August 6 with another show at Caesar's for which she was very grateful. "It's not so very easy to get a slot in Vegas, so it's taken a long time. This is really a special thing. I'm very, very excited about it." She really liked the idea of going back to her hotel room after the performance rather than getting on a bus and touring to the next city. "For the last two years, I've been thinking: Wouldn't it be great if I could play Vegas once in a while? Because when you travel, a lot of your energy really goes into your travel. Packing, unpacking."

While Vegas continues to be one of Stevie's favorite cities, she was almost seriously injured during a show there several years ago. She played a private concert at the Hard Rock for the clothing company Kenneth Cole. At the end of the show, she fell dangerously backward over a bass amplifier. Stevie's bass player, Don Boyette, caught her but it was clearly a startling moment. "Those are the things you don't forget. I almost did break my neck."[1]

In a radio interview with Joe Benson of KLOS Radio in Los Angeles, Stevie explained that when she and Waddy Wachtel went to see Elton John and Celine Dion's shows at Caesar's Palace, they realized how stupid it would look if they stood in the middle of a 110-foot-wide stage with just the band. "It's bigger than the biggest stadium stage. We've nicknamed the band 'The Flea Circus'—we're afraid we'll look like fleas onstage because of the hugeness of it."[2] They immediately went home to sort through old videos and clips to choose which would be a part of the show. "Elton John," she said, "has been filming himself since the age of 15."

In addition, the set included some of her favorite songs such as "How Still My Love" and "If Anyone Falls." "This is a chance for me to go back through all those many, many years and pick out a few songs I haven't always done. It's always exciting to do some new music."[3]

Stevie planned to take the summer off after she'd finished the Vegas shows. After all, she spent much of 2004 on tour with Fleetwood Mac and spent early 2005 assembling her Vegas show. "It was pretty fabulous, if I do say so myself," she joked in an interview with Bill Picture of the *San Francisco Chronicle*. As soon as Nicks cleared her calendar, unpacked, and began to settle back into life in Paradise Valley, Don Henley called to invite her to join him for ten co-headlining dates prior to his summer tour with the Eagles. "And when Don Henley asks you to rock with him, you don't say no. Plus, I thought, 'Well, I have this amazing show left over [from Vegas].' So I said, 'Ah, what the hell, let's do it.'"

Stevie and her band were on a roll. They continued their summer tour, adding Vanessa Carlton as the opening act. "I know her pretty well, and I just think she's a special one and I'm glad to be able to put her in front of a lot of people. My audiences are so excellent and so caring and loving, and I want her to feel that," Nicks added. "I believe these artists have to get out in front of the people. The music business is in such bad shape. Those artists don't get nurtured. It's frightening. We had people to nurture us," she said of the early part of her career when she teamed up with guitarist Lindsey Buckingham. "We had a producer who let us live in his house. We had people around us who would say, 'Don't get upset' and 'We'll keep you afloat.' In this day and age, it's 'Get out.' I really respect her. I'll be damned if I'll let her go by the wayside. She is one of the great ones. She won't quit."[4]

Vanessa obviously had Stevie feeling nostalgic. "I adore that girl, but I can't watch her because I get all choked up. Vanessa reminds me so much of myself at that age. You know, Lindsey and I were very much in love, and I had this intense passion for [making music]. I cry because she makes me remember why I started doing this."[5]

When asked about her summer tour by Joe Benson of KLOS Radio in Los Angeles, Stevie, in her exceedingly confident way, told him that she and Waddy Wachtel "put their heart and soul into it." She described it as "so rockin," despite their respective ages of fifty-seven and fifty-eight, and said it "fills your soul and keeps you young." They have been friends since she and Lindsey met him in 1971. Waddy knew her when she was a cleaning lady and doing lunch at the steak house. The first encore they played during the late summer tour was Led Zeppelin's "Rock and Roll." Stevie described it as "the high point of the night." In her valley-girl style she quipped, "It's like Oh My God! It's so much fun. It's rockin'. It's shades of Led Zeppelin."

But when Stevie returned home to Paradise Valley after the summer tour, she faced one of the biggest losses of her life. She wrote about it to her fans on *nicksfix.com*. "My father died today [August 10, 2005] at 3:06pm. He was a force of nature. He waited until the Fleetwood Mac Tour was over—I asked him for that. He waited until this summer tour was over—I asked him for that. He couldn't leave us during a tour—he knew that. The last show was Saturday in Vegas. I got here to Phoenix Sunday night. It is Wednesday night. He waited for me."

According to the *East Valley Tribune*, her father, Jess Nicks, eighty, "owned and operated now-defunct Valley outdoor concert venue Compton Terrace south of Phoenix. He had also been the chairman of the board of the Arizona Heart Foundation for three decades and had suffered from heart disease since 1974, undergoing three open heart operations."

Stevie with Don Henley, Philadelphia—June 3, 2005
(Photo by Mandy Gossett)

Stevie with Sharon Celani, Philadelphia—June 3, 2005
(Photo by Mandy Gossett)

Thirteen

The Mad Songwriter

Stevie, though widely known for her distinctive voice, sees herself first as a songwriter: "When I joined Fleetwood Mac, I didn't think I was a lead singer. I have a strange voice, a hard voice to get accepted—that's why I always considered myself a writer and not a singer. Only in the last couple of years have I begun to think I could sing.

"If I did it all over again I would probably do the same thing. I love my music. I am really more interested in becoming a really great songwriter and you know, doing other things in this world besides being a mother and having children and being in a marriage. You know, it's just not my priority."[1]

When asked by Ian "Molly" Meldrum of ABC Australia who most influenced her when she was writing her first song at the age of sixteen, Stevie said, "Everly Brothers, I would say The Beatles except for the fact when I met Lindsey he was so insistent that I listen to The Beatles for form, for like, here's your verse, here's your one bar, and I'm going, this is a bar down the corner—right? I mean, two bars, and then there's another verse, and then you have to have a chorus, and now you have to have a bridge, and I'm going over to a blotter, and I don't understand this, so I got a little upset with people that I was forced to listen to.

"So, I was not forced to listen to the Everly Brothers and I was not forced to listen to R&B or The Supremes or The Beach Boys, The Four Tops. Somewhere between The Beatles and the Kingston Trio I kind of burned out a little bit and said in my own self, quietly, 'I'm going and find what I want to sing and listen to, even though I'll sing what you want me to do when I'm with you. But in my own private time I'm going to sing to Diana Ross and I'm going to sing to Aretha Franklin, that's just the way it is.'"

Stevie explained in 1981 that Joni Mitchell also had a big influence on her songwriting. "I've written for years and been influenced by lots of people, but I guess the stuff that really got me was Joni Mitchell's early songs. I learned so much from listening to her. In fact, I probably wouldn't be doing this if it hadn't been for her. It was her music that showed me I could say everything I wanted to and push it into one sentence and sing it well. *Ladies of the Canyon* taught me a lot. I remember lying on the floor, listening to Joni's records, studying every single word. When she came out with a new album I'd go crazy—'Don't bother me this week. I'm listening to Joni Mitchell.'"[2]

Perhaps the most honest and touching assessment of Stevie's songwriting came from Christine McVie in the *Classic Albums: Rumours* DVD. "Stevie's words can be pretty obscure…at best. Sometimes I didn't know what she was singing about, but in her mind those words made complete sense and I often used to wonder what on earth she was talking about. But then, you didn't care because the words just sounded so good."

"I have so many songs that that would drive me nuts! I write constantly," Stevie told *Revolution*. "I'll be sitting at the piano, writing, and Christine [McVie] will walk past me and she'll go, 'It's the mad songwriter again, writing another song. You've got so many songs. I don't know why you're doing this!' And I say, 'Christine, because I just love to do it, and it's really important to me to get whatever it is that I'm writing out, even if nobody ever hears it.' There are a lot of songs I've written that are really good, but just never made it onto a record."

What inspires Stevie Nicks? "I'm inspired by life, I'm inspired by people. If I fix up a room with some nice candles and put some beautiful things around, I can usually sit down at the typewriter or with a journal and write. I think it's all about environment. You can change your environment and change your whole mood. If you're not happy, then you just have to pack a bag and go somewhere else. There's nothing like it to bring out the creative side of you. I just throw some stuff in a duffel bag and take off…"[3]

Stevie's Paradise Valley home also serves as inspiration for her writing. "It's fabulous, not because there's a lot of expensive stuff in it but because of all the neat stuff I've collected since I was in high school," she told *Rolling Stone*. "There's a lamp that my mom bought for me when I first joined Fleetwood Mac. It's a blue Tiffany lamp, dark blue, and it's called the blue lamp. I keep a fireplace burning, even when it's 99 degrees. I just turn the air-conditioning up. My mother goes crazy. She says, 'Do you know how much money you spend to keep this house cool and then you burn fires in every single room? You're so weird Stevie.' Fire creates ambience. I need that fire. So back off, Mom."

Stevie uses her music to express the elements of her personality. "All the characters in my songs; The Gypsies, the Saras, and on this album [*The Other Side of the Mirror*], Alice and Juliet, they're all me. But they're all different sides of me. It's a great way to write about what's going on in your life without telling it in a real serious way, but the point comes over and I think people understand that."[4]

"Once I write a song that connects with people; they don't ever forget that connection. So I think a lot of connections were made in the very, very beginning that made it last through now. Because those were such strong ties that were made then, that they just were never broken." Mick Fleetwood added, "She has an audience that is incredibly forgiving where things have gone wrong for Stevie and I'm talking about times when she didn't remember that she was walking out on stage, you know. Which is my God, not the case now. They literally adore her; it's as simple as that."[5] Her connection with the fans continues to grow as she tours as a solo artist. Stevie has become so much more comfortable speaking with her audience. She never got a chance to talk onstage with Fleetwood Mac. Lindsey Buckingham didn't like it!

Stevie discussed her thoughts about being a gay icon for *Borders.com*. "I think that my music, when I write it, I want it to be for everyone, if you're gay or not gay or whatever, this music is for you. That's my way of teaching. If I hadn't been who I am now I would be a teacher and I would be somehow teaching with my music. I would have figured a way to work the music into what I did at school. So when I do this now I feel like I get to share my philosophies on the world and love and how we get through life and what is making us happy, what's not, how to move on, and that's what I try to do. The fact I have made a connection with the world in the way I have is really amazing and I feel really blessed for that."

On the differences between Lindsey's songwriting and her own, *BAM* magazine captured the essence in 1981. "People don't mind a little misery, but they also like happy endings. It's nice to leave some hope at the end that things will work out. See, Lindsey won't do that. He'll say, 'Go your own way,' I wouldn't, most likely. Lindsey hates to write lyrics, though. Maybe that's why some of his songs are so negative. He'll have all these beautiful songs that are instrumentals for months. They have gorgeous melodies, layer upon layer of guitars. I exercise to his tapes, practice ballet to them. Then he'll write lyrics for this beautiful song and it'll have a different feeling than the music."

It seems surprising that Lindsey and Stevie have not collaborated on songs since she is such a lyricist and he enjoys the musical component. "I'm surprised, too. I always wanted to. It's strange. You would think he would ask me, but I think he really doesn't like my lyrics very much. They're too spacey for him. We think differently, I guess. Lindsey and I have so much behind us that it would be difficult to sit down and intensely get into lyrics. As it is he asks me, 'Who's that one about? What are you talking about in that line? What does that mean?'"[6]

"When I started out, some writers called me a sex symbol. I always pointed out that I was a songwriter. If you want to stay in this business, you better write your own songs, because any career built on being cute is doomed. Nobody stays cute forever."[7] Stevie has maintained her appeal, however, and was even listed in *AARP Magazine's* 2005 Hot Fifty List in the "Coolest Crooner" category.

"I think being blatantly sexy is stupid and it wears off. If that's what your fame is built on, you're dead in the water." Her I-won't-sell-sex stance extends past her sartorial choices. Nicks won't entertain writing overtly sexual lyrics even at the behest of colleagues like Prince, who, she said, "would've liked to have dated me at one time." When Prince made the mistake of suggesting Nicks turn up the heat in her music, she recalled telling him, "'You have to write about sex, so you must not be intrinsically sexy. I don't have to write about sex because I am intrinsically sexy.' That shut his mouth right up."[8]

In addition to being the front woman for Fleetwood Mac, Stevie created an image. When Maggie Bruber asked her to what degree the tambourine had contributed to her image, she had this to say, "Actually, that began a long time ago. I first really started playing tambourine in Fleetwood Mac when I realized that when you're one of three singers and you have pretty much equal amount of songs each, that means you don't have anything to do for two thirds of the set. So I figured I needed to find something to do to make me look valid up there, so I really started playing the tambourine. And I figured it needed to be decorated in some way like the chiffon and stuff in my skirts, so that it would move around and I would create a little bit of twirly picture from head to toe. So we started putting the long ribbons and feathers on. Many, many incarnations of the tambourine, sometimes ribboning, sometimes velvet stuff, whatever. And the microphone stand too."

Stevie confessed her real fear when asked why she doesn't play the guitar during concerts by *High Times* in 1982. "I'm not good enough. There's no reason. If I was terrific, then maybe they'd find a part for me, but I'm not, so it would be for the look of it, and I'd be too nervous. I'd be so nervous, it wouldn't look or sound good and then everybody would be mad at me, and Lindsey would be screaming at me that it was out of tune. And I don't need that for sure."

The mechanics of writing are different for all songwriters, as Stevie explained for Jenny Boyd's *Musicians in Tune*. "I go from writing in my journal to typing out some ideas on the typewriter. It's really fun for me because I just put on music that I like that's got a good beat and makes me feel good and then I type along to the beat. I just read the words and put it into rhyme and then I'll take that paper to the piano and just start writing, and it either happens or it doesn't. Usually if I get it pretty complete on the paper before I get to the piano, then it's usually real easy. If I go to the piano without anything, with just an empty piece of paper and a pencil, then it's harder. But I do that sometimes. I just sit down and play a chord and I'll just write a line, like say, 'the white winged dove,' then I'll play a chord, or a couple of chords and I'll start humming something."

Stevie remembers writing every song she's created. She writes a song structure inside of ten minutes, then spends days playing it and editing it. She always starts with lyrics, and then usually moves to piano with a song component or sometimes to guitar to work out instrument parts. "Every once in a while I'll go to a piano without a poem, but usually I have a full-on, formal stanza poem, and I go and sit down at the piano, and I put on a recorder and record it. And usually, the very first thing out of my mouth is the best thing. I don't ever go back and change anything. And if somebody suggests I change something, I don't have a very good reaction to that. Songs penned on piano are generally more intricate than songs written on guitar, unless you're Eric Clapton."[9]

Because she wasn't properly trained, Nicks used to suffer vocal problems from singing. But she's been taking better care of her vocal chords for nine years. "I do 40 minutes of exercises three hours before I walk onstage every single show, and I've been doing that since 1997," she told Elfman. "It's like going to the gym every day. You go to a vocal coach, and you study, and you go through every vowel sound, and you work with your vocal chords so they're all stretched out, like a ballerina would do, or a Vegas showgirl would do."

Stevie's intent is to provide her fans with more than mere music. "What a writer wants to do is put stuff out there and make people mull it over in their minds until suddenly it's something that's way more important than turning on the stereo."[10] In May of 1998, Stevie explained how therapeutic writing can be for Jim Moret of *CNN Showbiz Weekly This Week*. "My songwriting has always been an outlet for me, because it does allow you to put down on paper—first it goes down on paper, you know—how you're feeling. And I think once you put it down on paper and look at it down there, it becomes easier to deal with."

Stevie's efforts have not gone unnoticed. She was honored with the Blockbuster Artistic Achievement in Songwriting award in 2001. Her acceptance speech came straight from the heart and, as always, was quite endearing. "Since this award is for songwriting, I wanted to say a little bit to you, very quickly, about songwriting. In 1975 when I first joined Fleetwood Mac, I really thought, how am I going to plan this out? I'm gonna plan it, and I did, I planned it and I decided to try to make little worlds for you guys to come with me into for a little while, and I think that is what I love the most about my writing. So I thank you all for coming into that little world with me, even if it's just for a minute of your time, and being with me because that's what I do. I love you and thank you so much."

Fourteen

What's Next?

One might think Stevie has done it all, but she apparently still has more to accomplish. "I will someday write my autobiography, she told *Entertainment Weekly* in 1998, but I can't until we're all—me and Don Henley and the other people who were in my life—70 years old and we don't care anymore. When nobody's wife will be mad at me. My story is not a dirty, nasty story; when I tell it, I want it to be wonderful, and I don't want anybody to be hurt by it. When I'm 65, that's when I'll be able to write my book. When I do my next boxed set."

Stevie believes her book will be much better than other Fleetwood Mac members. "Mick [Fleetwood] is writing a book, and my book is gonna be much better than his book, because I've been writing this for 15 years. I'll bury his book with my book, and he knows it. And he won't let me read his book. So I told him, 'Mick, if you slander me, babe, I'll bury you. I will write down everything that you have ever done and put it out.' We've been laughing about this for a week, because his book is coming out in about three months, and he still hasn't let one person in the band see it. It's turned into kind of a joke at this point. But it will not be a joke if this book comes out and I don't like what's in it. So I simply told him, 'Well, I'll sue you. I'll just sue you for everything that you have, and then you'll just be poor and penniless again, and you'll be sorry.' I'm laughing the whole time that I'm saying this and he's laughing, but we're really very serious."[1]

Stevie also told *USA Today* in 2001 that she intends to write the book but not until she is much older. "I've had a completely wild, crazy and exotic life, and I absolutely want to tell that outrageous story," Nicks said. "I'll write it when I'm 90. I'm not comfortable doing it now, because all the people are still alive—and married. It would be a shame to change the names."

"Even the bad stuff is interlaced with the good, so it wouldn't be just one depressing monologue. It's a fabulous story. A Cinderella story for all of us, not just me."[2]

Stevie is notorious for her journaling. She even shares parts of them with fans on *nicksfix.com*. Her 9/11 journals brought comfort to many who read them. They are full of all her experiences clear back to the early days and will be the basis for her autobiography. "I have journals all the way back to the beginning of Fleetwood Mac. The Klonopin journals are not so good."[3] The *Baltimore Sun* captured Stevie's secret to journaling. "We didn't get in until real late last night, until probably about four, and I typed for about three hours. I was so tired that I would put my head down on the typewriter and almost go to sleep, and then I'd wake back up and I'd type another couple paragraphs. I go home from every tour with a binder full of journalistic prose of the tour, and then also a lot of poetry. They [the band] don't know that I'm writing this every night, I don't show them until the end of the tour. Then I have it bound into a little book, and I give it to everybody."

Drawing and painting are passions of Stevie's that she also plans to continue. "Sulamith Wülfing lives on the edge of the Black Forest in Germany," she told *MTV* in 1983. "That's how I learned to draw. When my friend Robin got sick, I wanted to send her something of myself to hang on the wall. For ten years, I'd had all these Sulamith Wülfing books. I draw like her—even though she is incredible, and I'm not—but the initial spirit comes from her. All these years on the road, I'd look at her drawings, late after concerts, and get a lot of comfort from them. I think she's probably a lot like me. The world kind of scares her and freaks her out, and she just wants to do this one thing, and she did it."

While Stevie has continued to write and perform music longer than she may have expected, she also has plans to share her paintings. "My mom says that God will never give you more than you can handle, and I really try to believe this, because sometimes I think that I've been given more than I can handle. But it seems that I do have a real instinct to survive, and I'm way too proud to let anything stop me or get in my way.

"And I have way too many things to do on this Earth to let anything stop me. I want to write a book, and I want to do my paintings and get them out to the world. And that's what I'll do in another 10 years when I decide to really stop what I'm doing right now."[4] In fact, she's said she'd like to do a book of art and poetry, all of which have been common themes over the last few years. "I do [still paint]. That's just something that's there, and one day the time will be right and I'll do a coffee-table book. It's just sitting there waiting, like the next album."[5] Poets Stevie enjoys include Oscar Wilde and Edgar Allan Poe.

More recently in 2001 for *Spotlight on Stevie Nicks*, she further elaborated on her plans. "I don't really call myself a painter...I draw. So I draw my pictures and then sometimes I paint them in and sometimes I don't. So I'm really more into the fine drawing...And I just draw little creatures, and little people and little bits of my drawing has gone out over the years...I'm doing...I'm gonna do a book...I'm working on it now with my best friend. That's just art...art and some poetry and some little vignettes from my journals that I think are going to be really nice. And it'll be in the next year or two...so you'll get to actually see what I draw, because I've been doing this always, I've just never shown anybody. My drawing is like my meditation."

In addition to her autobiography and artwork, Stevie has stated an intention to pursue a movie project based on an acclaimed series of fantasy stories featuring the character Rhiannon from Welsh mythology. She is not a stranger to the Hollywood scene, given her contributions on several soundtracks such as "Edge of Seventeen" (*School of Rock*), "If You Ever Did Believe" and "Crystal" (*Practical Magic*), "Somebody Stand By Me" (*Boys on the Side*), "Touched by an Angel" (*Sweet November*), "Violet and Blue" (*Against All Odds*), "Sleeping Angel" (*Fast Times at Ridgemont*

High), Tom Petty's "Free Fallin'" (*Party of Five*), "Sorcerer" (*Streets of Fire*), "Blue Lamp" (*Heavy Metal*), "Battle of the Dragon" (*American Anthem*) and "Twisted" with Lindsey Buckingham (*Twister*). Stevie, along with the other members of Fleetwood Mac, received a star on Hollywood's Walk of Fame in October of 1979.

As for Fleetwood Mac, which played nearly 140 shows in support of the 2003 comeback album *Say You Will*, Nicks told Jonathan Cohen of *Billboard.com* in 2004, "We're just resting right now, because we feel that as all wonderful things go, you come out and you make a big show of it, and then you go away for a little bit and rest, so when you come back, it's all wonderful again."

In February and March, 2006, Stevie took her Gold Dust tour to Australia and New Zealand, performing her Vegas show with help from the Melbourne Symphony Orchestra and John Farnham. While in Australia promoting her tour, Stevie attended the Victorian (Horse) Racing Carnival and even had The Stevie Nicks Stakes race named in her honor. She was stressed out for days prior to her trip, searching the Internet for hours to ensure she had the right hats and clothes for the event. She would also like to sing with some of the great singers like Barbra Streisand, Robert Plant, and Aretha Franklin someday. And it is also likely she'll continue to perform in Las Vegas for quite some time. "So, for me, as an almost 57-year-old woman, this looks very good, because it means you can put all of your energy into the show as opposed to traveling all over the United States. It would be a nice thing for me to be able to do [Vegas] until I'm a very old, little old lady."[6] While songwriting is her passion, it's unclear how she will proceed with releasing her music. "It's like, does it really matter at this point?" she told Guy Beckman in Australia when asked if she is working on a follow-up to her last solo album, 2001s *Trouble In Shangri-La*. "Do people really want to hear a whole other solo record, when you can get one or two songs from iTunes? I'm thinking about a way you could just put out a few songs once in a while, maybe four songs that you loved, instead of having to figure out 16 songs, many of which you might not love." Other projects Stevie has been planning over the years include a ballet of her ten-song opus of "Rhiannon" and the release of her children's books entitled *A Goldfish and a Ladybug* and *The Golden Fox Of The Last Fox Hunt.* She once told *Hit Parader* magazine about even more goals. "I think it would be fun to make a record for children. You can teach kids an incredible amount through music. I'd also like to record an album of songs by my grandfather, AJ Nicks, who was a country singer."

Stevie works hard to maintain her rock 'n' roll status and never wants to disappoint her fans. She's also learned to relax and enjoy life a bit more. "In the old days I used to get up at 5. Now I'm up by 11 to watch my soaps: *All My Children, One Life to Live,* and *General Hospital.* For years, this has been my top priority."[7] Many women believe soap operas create a depressive mood since they often portray unrealistic romantic relationships. That could be a contributing factor in Stevie's tendency to write songs wrought with melancholy and anger. That, however, may be changing.

After 18 months away from songwriting while touring the world, Stevie has finally put pen to paper. The new song is an ode to New Orleans, as yet untitled, but bound to wring a few more drops of emotion from the hurricane-battered city. "I'm in the middle of writing a happy song—not a sad song—about the plight of New Orleans. I have so many memories of New Orleans because we always play there. I'm not gonna write a really miserable song," she ruefully declared. "I'm going to write a song about the New Orleans that was—and hopefully will come again."[8]

While Stevie does have what some would call a magical life, she does not have a lifelong romantic partner. She tends to be a bit defensive about it, attributing the conundrum to her chosen lifestyle. "I live in the world of romantic possibilities. My soul mate could be right around the next corner. He is out there. My mother promised me that. I'm a free spirit. I don't want a boss asking me when I'm going to be home. Most men think the way I live my life is crazy."[9]

"If I meet somebody, that's great," she said. "But if that doesn't happen I'm not lonely. I'm happy and I have lots of fun by myself. I'm not looking for somebody to fill up my life." Even losing her father has not eliminated the hard-earned serenity. "I have had a very easy time with it, and the reason is that he did 55 of those 135 Fleetwood Mac shows with us," she said.

"He had such a great time, he had a little electric scooter and he was buzzing all over the venues."

Six months after the end of the 2003 Fleetwood Mac tour, her father joined her again on a short U.S. solo tour with Don Henley. But this time things were very different. Despite pleas from his friends and family to stay home, Jess, ever so devoted to his daughter, was absolutely going because Stevie wanted him there.

"I said out loud to everybody, 'In my heart I really wish that he would just go on to the next plane, because he is not having fun. He doesn't feel well, he can't buzz around in his scooter any more, someone is wheeling him around in a wheelchair, and he is hating it.'"

The next night, Jess Nicks fell in his hotel room. A week later, he was gone. "I really took it with the grace he would have wanted. I feel he pushes me towards the beauty in my life. So it's been OK. I'm not sad, I'm just glad that he's not in pain any more."[10]

Stevie is at her best. Strong, grateful and continuing to make sure her life matters.

Her avoidance of relationships has likely protected her in some respects. "I haven't had a terrible marriage. I don't have children who are on drugs and who are refusing to call me. Because of that, I can go back to that childhood innocence we all have. Then I can make up these little romantic worlds for people to come into and hang out. That's why I make my records, to take people away from their lives for a while."[11]

Mick Fleetwood, a former lover and soul mate, said it best. "Her child is her career or, you know, she loves what she does. She absolutely loves it. And she gets nervous and she gets fretted out. I think she'll be doing this for donkey's years, because she has a loyalty to that."[12]

She does have some misgivings about her decisions over the years. "My biggest regret is that I didn't have better money people that watched out for me," she told *myLAUNCH*, "which is the old story that you hear from the movie stars from 1920, right? I wish I had a better money person, I wish I had somebody that I would listen to more, so that I would've saved the incredible fortune that I made—which isn't to say I don't have any money. I do, I have lots of money. But I don't have a lot of the money that

I should have, because I just blew it, you know? And now I'm real sorry that I did that. I would've liked to have had that in the bank, or had another house—or given it to charity or something. So that makes me really sad, but...hey, it's gone. And we had a good time!!"

Patriotism is a strong thread in Stevie's life. She has written to the troops and even visited the war injured at Walter Reed Army Medical Center, bringing them T-shirts and 450 iPods programmed with music from her and niece Jessica's personal collection. After her visit, she wrote this in her journal. "I look at life through the eyes of a rock and roll fairy princess who lives for nothing more than to sing a song—break a few hearts—and fly on to the next city and do it all again...until today. I walked into Walter Reed today a single woman with no children. I walked out a mother, a wife, a girlfriend, a sister, a daughter, a nurse, a patient's advocate—a changed woman. What I saw today will never leave my heart. The boys of Iraq (and a few older ones, too). And the families—the father who showed me the shrapnel they took out of his son and then took his medals and laid them at his child's feet—such a beautiful father...in so much pain, but always hopeful his son will make it and I believe that..."

Community service is also important to Stevie. Hurricane relief aid has been a priority with Stevie performing on the *Today Show* in September of 2005 on behalf of the NBC, Warner Brothers Music, and the Habitat for Humanity project. She also personally delivered lunch to a group of fire-fighters after the 9/11 terrorist attacks in New York. At the encouragement of John Kinney, the web master for *nicksfix.com,* 1,395 of her fans and Senator Kay Bailey Hutchison, a flag was flown over the U.S. Capitol in honor of Stevie's patriotism on February 14, 2003. The flag was ultimately presented to her along with a plaque and the names of her supportive fans.

Doug Elfman captured Stevie's gratefulness for what she's accomplished during a 2005 interview with the *Las Vegas Review Journal.* "There's a lot of little Rhiannons out there, and I met them when they were babies. And now they're all grown up. It's pretty trippy to go back into Madison, Wisconsin and meet a little girl that you picked up and swung around onstage when she was 1, and now she's 25. But I feel pretty blessed. I feel like there were angels just taking me through all this and letting me have such an amazing success. I appreciate it every day. I don't take it for granted."

Stevie has not shed her love for the mystical. "I don't think there's anything funny at all about my love of ethereal things or magic or the spirit world. I'm very serious about those things."[13] When asked if she is surprised that she lived through it all, she had this to say. "I am amazed. I feel very lucky. If I had not caught that Klonopin thing, I am absolutely sure I would have been dead in a year—no doubt in my mind. I feel really lucky that somebody tapped me on the shoulder—some little spirit—and said, 'You know what? You better go to a hospital right now and get better.'"[14]

On why mysticism has always been a part of her work, Stevie justified her beliefs for *Interview* magazine. "Because having a little bit of the spiritual is ultimately better than having none…A long, long time ago I decided I was going to have a kind of mystical presence, so I made my clothes, my boots, my hair, and my whole being go with that. But it wasn't something I just made up at that point. It's the way I've always been. I've always believed in good witches—not bad witches—and fairies and angels."

Having spent some time involved with the Episcopal church as a child, she has remained in touch with her faith. "I am religious. I wasn't raised in any religion, because we were always moving when I was a kid and didn't get involved in any church. But I believe there have been angels with me constantly through these last 20 years, or I wouldn't be alive. I pray a lot. In the last few years I've asked for things from God, and he's given them to me. And there were things I thought were gonna kill me, and he fixed them…I was destroying this gift that God gave me and asked for help. Now I'm happy, even outside my music, and enjoying my life."[15]

Stevie refers to her home as commune-like in that many types of people have come and lived there for a time. Where it was once a rock 'n' roll party haven, it is now quite calm. If it wasn't already obvious that Stevie is a generous and loving person from her lyrics and relentless dedication to her family, friends, and fans, it is apparent in her transformation from the rock 'n' roll lifestyle to a peaceful family-oriented existence—where she remains, surrounded by the people who knew her before the stardom.

Just imagine as Stephanie Tuck conducted her 2002 interview for *In Style* magazine, Jessica, then ten years old, twirling in a gypsy-like frock doing her best Aunt Stevie impression without really knowing what all that "spinning in place" really means. Stevie could only laugh, saying, "Oh boy, here we go again."

Her concerts remain sold out and applause abounds when Stevie does her trademark "spinning in place" during songs such as "Stand Back." Concert reviewers no longer perceive her spinning as Stevie stoned and tormented, but rather, Stevie, rock star icon, appreciating and enjoying her life with family, friends, and her pets while making music, traveling, and "giving back" her priorities.

Stevie—"Spinning in place"
(Source: www.catanna.com / steviephotos.htm)

Rhiannon artwork Stevie created for
Robin Anderson
(Source: http://inherownwords.com)

Rhiannon painting Stevie created for
City of Hope Leukemia Foundation
(Source: http://inherownwords.com)

Fifteen

The Fan Connection

Through her music, Stevie gives you herself. Her fans feel a deep connection to her music, to her travails and to her personal conquests. Her battles have helped them through their battles. Her music has counseled them, motivated them, and consoled them in their times of greatest need.

"Words cannot adequately express the way I feel about Stevie or the positive influence she's had on my life. At times, Stevie and her music has been all that has kept me alive. I grew up in the San Diego County, California foster care system, eventually surviving close to 19 years worth of verbal, physical, and sexual abuse. There were many times when I thought I'd not last even one moment longer, so great were the physical and psychic pain that wracked my very heart and soul. It sounds overly dramatic, but, especially as a youngster I thought that some sort of romanticized death by my own hand would be preferable to the real-life-hell I perceived myself to be living in. Often, it would be only Nicks' lyrics (or, rather, my sad, teenaged version of what they represented to me) that kept me from attempting to "do myself in" yet again. The hope of fulfilling an old childhood dream, to meet Miss Nicks herself and to let her know just how much her words, her artwork, her grace, style, presentation, fortitude, and voice have meant to me over time and have helped me through many, many more suicidal spots in my tumultuous adulthood. (Erica Vanessa Fox, San Diego County, CA)

"For certain, there is no short explanation or definition of how important Stevie has been to me and to my daughters. For a fact, I could not have survived my life without her. She is a legend and at the same time so down to earth. A "real kindred spirit." Stevie's songs over the past three decades have pulled me out of depression, given me the strength to fight for my children and the courage to do the right thing at all cost. To this day her music captivates, motivates, inspires, encourages and helps me get through the rough times of life, love and relationships. It helps me understand who I am. She connects me. She grounds me. She makes me smile." (Gayle Rickert)

"Stevie's music has inspired me for a long time. The thing that sticks out in my mind the most, is when my aunt was diagnosed with cancer, I turned to Stevie's music for peace. Peace is exactly what it brought me. There is one specific song that touched me the most—the song "Touched by an Angel." No matter how upset I was while my aunt was dying, I listened to this song and felt comfort. Stevie has inspired me to be myself and not try to fit into a mold that doesn't suit me." (Heather Clough)

Even the younger generation relates to Stevie Nicks. Facing some of the same challenges as Stevie and the younger musicians she mentors, they find comfort in knowing that she made it through all the painful situations, moving above all the adversity to reach even higher levels of success and happiness.

"Stevie Nicks has been my role model for 4–5 years. I am only 15 but I love Stevie Nicks. She has inspired me more than ever." (Caitlin)

"I first heard Stevie Nicks's voice on the radio when I was fifteen. I am now twenty one. I was totally into country at the time but I had to find out more about that voice so I did research and got some CDs. Now I am in a rock band of my own...all thanks to the inspiration of Miss Stephanie Nicks." (Barbra McGuire, Middletown, OH)

"It was April 13th 2002 when I was converted to the world of Stevie Nicks! 'The bright light was lying down...the earth the sea and the sky...'...those words did me in! When I heard this song [Planets of the Universe] for the first time, I started to cry. I had never heard such raw power and emotion in any song before. At this point in my life, 18 years of age, I was struggling with typical teenage issues—trying to find who I was and battling pressures of society. Listening to this "angelic" voice made me feel safe...secure! I began doing research on Stevie Nicks as I didn't know a whole lot about her. When I read various interviews and stories about her life and past experiences and struggles with issues that were similar to mine, I began to think, 'Hey, she survived! If she can make it through so can I!!!' Stevie Nicks, in my opinion, is the strongest person I know of. It is her strength and will with which I feed to keep going...keep alive." (Sándor Molnar)

"I was inspired by Stevie in a very dark way. Someone died in a very bad way and I saw it and didn't know how to deal with my emotions. It was overwhelming sadness. I ran down a flight of stairs, up the hall and went into the room and put on someone's cassette. "Kind of Woman" came on. I calmed down. I danced and I don't dance! All fate changed. My failures at the present were gone. It didn't matter. I found a solution and realized what I was meant to do. Money didn't matter or prestige. My career was going to change before I even started. So young—almost eighteen. I do direct care now which is so different from my past decision. Thank you Stevie. My life is great despite the "Storms." You helped with the "Landslide" and I help people partly because of you." (Jean-marie Andrejack, Point Pleasant, NJ)

"Stevie's music has really impacted my life. My dad has heart disease and when I found out how much Stevie has done for heart disease medical research I was very happy. Her dad had heart problems too so I feel like I am not the only one who worries for my dad. Being that I am only 16 years old, my dad is a major part of my life and I don't know what I'd do without him. I just want to let you know how grateful I am for Stevie's contributions to

heart research. Every time my dad is hospitalized due to his heart, I know that I can look to Stevie and her family for inspiration." (Jessica Marshalek, Sarver, PA)

Equally important is the balance she helps provide in our lives. After many years of searching and experimentation, Stevie knows who she is and what she wants. Her artistry coupled with her life's achievements and experiences have impacted the lives of many in a unique, powerful and positive way. No artist is more revered for exuding such strength and warmth while maintaining an unparalleled audience connection. Tim Rigney of Syracuse, NY said it best. "Stevie is 'strange and elusive'—she's Rhiannon and once in a million years a lady like her rises—and yet—she's us—one of us."

"Stevie is an inspiration to all of us who wish to achieve success, overcome obstacles and make all of our goals a reality while leading a productive and happy life." (Glenn Weiden-Miller, Long Grove IL)

"Stevie is such a wonderful artist and a great songwriter who doesn't get the credit she deserves for all that she has done for the music industry." (Sue Bradford)

"Stevie has always been and always will be the Queen of Rock and Roll." (Cindi Dudley, Houston, TX)

"Stevie is a true legend and deserves everything she gets. More importantly, she has brought together two people who have shared a life together and continue to do so. We love Stevie and she is a superstar." (Dave & Ian, Sunderland, UK)

"Stevie Nicks is a true Poet, Priest of Nothing...Legend...

Listening to Stevie's music has given me a greater appreciation of musical artistry. The passion that goes into her writing, her performance, her fan-base, and her contributions to many organizations such as the Arizona Heart Foundation is just astounding. Not to mention Stevie's stage presence, which exudes not only power but a sort of sensuality rarely accomplished by an artist. She is one of few who have the ability to enchant an arena of thousands, have them wrapped around her little finger and sing a tune or twenty that actually have some meaning, some feeling.

Classic songs such as "Landslide" and "Storms," the entire Bella Donna album, and many more have helped me through some troubling times and given the right circumstances will bring tears to my eyes because I feel them as she and countless others feel them. While songs like "Gypsy," "Rooms On Fire," and "Stand Back" are just very easy songs to listen to and enjoy on a regular basis. The fact that all of her songs come straight from the heart and from the life that she leads is truly awe-inspiring. All of them Beautiful. All of them Enchanting. It is for these reasons and more that Ms. Nicks continues to have an incredible impact on my life, and will for years upon years to come. Words just simply cannot express the gratitude I feel for the one and only Stevie Nicks." (Brandon Pollard, Kingston, Nova Scotia, Canada)

"I picked Stevie up at the airport in Dallas about twelve years ago. She was in town for a friend's wedding in Plano, TX. When I grabbed her luggage, I had already opened the back door of the limo but she asked me if she could ride in the front with me instead. I thought that was really cool. After the wedding, Stevie just wanted me to drive her around and show her the Dallas sights. She messed around with the radio, listening to music while we talked about my dogs. She just wanted to relax." (Alex Valdes, Dallas, TX)

"The first time I saw Stevie Nicks I was hooked. That was in the early '80s when I saw the video for "Stop Draggin My Heart Around." Since then, her music has guided me through life. It seems that at some of my biggest turning points one of her songs has been there but not by my choosing. It just plays. Live or recorded. A mystery to me just like her life. The night I met my husband he was standing by the jukebox selecting songs to play. After he was done, he moved across from the machine to the bar and I made my selections.

I stood next to him, we did not speak to each other but then "Rooms on Fire" played and he was singing along as was I. Then "Rooms on Fire" played again right after the first play. It turns out he picked it as his last selection and I picked it as my first. The day that I moved in with him, when I was still wondering if this was a good decision, I got into the car all packed and when I turned on the radio "Gypsy" came on. I went to see Stevie during the Trouble in Shangri-La tour and she ended the concert with "Has Anyone Ever Written Anything For You." I know it is a very moving song especially in concert but I was crying like a baby for no reason and I remember looking at my watch. When I got home there was a message on the answering machine from my mother telling me that my grandmother had just died and the stamp on the message was at the same time Stevie was singing "Has Anyone Ever Written Anything For You." I loved my grandmother. She actually raised me. But somehow maybe because I cried so much that night, who knows, Stevie comforted me and it was not as rough on me that my grandmother passed away. I love her music and many times I have sought comfort in it. Other times it creeps up on me which I do welcome because it makes me stronger, tougher and helps me understand that something good might be on its way for me or someone else." (Eff Henriquez, Abington, MA)

"In 1974 I walked by my older brother's room and heard a voice that was new to me. It was Stevie singing "Crystal" from the "Buckingham Nicks" album. I asked my brother if I could come in and listen. He said 'sure' and we continued to listen to the whole album together. I loved it so much I insisted on listening to it again. He looked at me with that "older brother look," smiled, grabbed his basketball and said 'see ya!' I got on the floor and listened to the album two more times. It was then I fell in love with Stevie's voice. My brother and his family moved far from mine several years ago. I helped him pack. When we came across the "Buckingham Nicks" album he smiled and gave it to me.

When Stevie joined Fleetwood Mac I fell in love with her songwriting. She takes us to her world through songs with such sophistication. To me, she is the rock and roll angel of shawls. For thirty years she has shared every emotion of my life. When you are in traffic coming home from work and you hear the first few notes of any Stevie song, you immediately smile, turn the volume up and enjoy the rest of the ride home. Stevie helps keep rock and roll alive. Oftentimes I'm sure people still ask Stevie what she thinks is her best written song. I don't think she could ever answer that. Her songwriting improves with each new album. The "Trouble in Shangri-La" album is my favorite of her solo collection. I'm happy for Stevie. She's in a good place right now and I'm excited to see what comes next." (Jen Shepp, Woodbridge, VA)

The persistence Stevie demonstrates is also emulated by many along with her love of the magical and mystical. People find Stevie and her music an escape from day-to-day stress and challenge. She soothes and entertains as she graciously shares her many life experiences. Stevie also serves as a female role model for strong women who have chosen a life of career over marriage and a family.

"Stevie's song lyrics have inspired me to keep going and never give up. I love the element of fairy tales and being in another world when listening to her songs!" (Jessica Fratelli, Pendell, PA)

"I can't get enough information about Stevie, the goddess of rock and roll. She has lived a life of destiny, one many of us can only dream about, and she has always graciously invited us in to share it with her. She is one of the few famous people who seem to genuinely love her fans. A rare jewel. It's a pleasure to listen to her music. One of my most favorite things in the world." (Tina Winstead)

"Stevie Nicks inspires me in a way that no other singer I have looked up to has. She is very much the 'Rock Mama'. She's beautiful, mystic, and very human and admits she's done some terrible things but turns them into something positive. One of the biggest reasons that I look up to her is because she hasn't sold out. She's a complete star. Nobody can touch her, she's very open with her feelings in everything she does, and she inspires me to go for my dreams, and do what I want to do with my life no matter what anyone says." (Monilara, Las Cruces, NM)

"Stevie to me is the classiest lady there is. She has a light that shines all around her and comes from inside her as well. I have related to her songs of the past and swear she has written them about my life. The album, The Other Side of the Mirror, *is one of those examples. I was in an abusive marriage, left and went back again and can really understand when she says in "Rhiannon," 'Your life knows no answer.' At one time I really felt that way and it is a frightening feeling when you think this is all your life is going to be about. Stevie writes what everyone feels (man or woman) at some point in their lives. She shows that she, too, has moments of sheer delight and enchantment and moments of deepest, darkest despair, that she is not immune to life. She has inspired much of my creativity (writing, drawing, etc.) in so many ways, I have created a website about her and my interests and when I was married on October 30, 2004, my wedding dress was inspired by and a tribute to her. The top of my dress was my own liking but the bottom and the colours were all Stevie. They were black, pink and ivory with a layered handkerchief hemline that we all love. The colours represent different "eras" of Stevie from the beginning years of Fleetwood Mac, to "Mirage" to "Bella Donna" and "The Wild Heart." Stevie was also the inspiration in me naming my daughter Stevie Lynn. I tell my Stevie that she doesn't need to dress the way some of these young ladies do. I tell her "look at Stevie Nicks. She dresses and acts like a lady and she still has men that would chew their arms off to be with her." I feel it has worked. She doesn't like to "show off" her body. I also tell my Stevie that if you believe in yourself and have something you really want to do, you can accomplish it just like Stevie Nicks did.*

Stevie, we listen to you and we listen through you. And the feeling does remain even after the glitter fades. We, your humble enchanted, gypsy fans, love you." (Dawn Benner)

"My sweetest memory of Stevie was New Year's Eve 2000 at the House of Blues in Las Vegas. I was on the production crew and had the honor of being her runner and green room server. I was fortunate to have met not only Stevie, but also her family. They were all the sweetest people!

I sculpt fairies, and in anticipation of her arrival, created a one-of-a-kind sculpture depicting Stevie as one of my fairies in the cloak she's wearing on the album "Timespace". Because the day was very hectic, I was holding on to it until the right moment to present it to her. When you work in this business, it's frowned upon to be too much of a fan because you're working. So I waited. And waited. I waited so long, that by the time I presented it to her, it was well after midnight and she was on her way back to her hotel for the evening. Even though it had been a long day—she had just played an awesome show, dealt with a meet and greet, and held court with all her visiting friends; she still spared a moment to talk with me. I explained that she had been a muse of mine over the years and that it would be my honor to share with her, the fruit of that inspiration. When I gave her the replica, she looked thoughtfully at it with a big smile on her face and in a childlike whisper said "I just love things like this!" She gave me the warmest hug and heartfelt thank you, bid me good night and went up to her room. Later I was told that she looked at the sculpture in detail the whole elevator ride up. That made me smile and still does today." (Suzanne Lugano)

"Stevie Nicks. The name conjures up images of a mystical musical pixie dancing on stage, twirling in chiffon, and giving all of herself to her music, her song, for her fans. She was creative and talented and worked very hard. She was strong, yet feminine. She was the first famous woman that did not give up her dreams or her ambitions for a man. She had love affairs, sang about the heartbreak but moved on. She never gave up her career or put it on the back burner for a man or a family. She showed that a woman can have a career and did not have to get married and have children to be happy and fulfilled. She stood on her two platform boots and rocked as hard as a man. She managed to not only have a successful solo career but to stay in Fleetwood Mac and thrive there as well. Not a small accomplishment at all.

I don't know exactly how to put it into words. I have always felt that connection to Stevie and her songs. I love how she writes. Poetic, physical, intuitive, and with heart and emotion. She paints a picture of her words to give you the deeper meaning behind the lyrics. With Stevie, I always know there is a story that is more than just words. She speaks, but the meaning behind the phrasing depicts what she is really saying between her lines. She invites me into her world when I listen to her music. And for a short time, I too am a creative, inspired woman. She lets me get a glimpse and imagine a life I could never have. A life of artistic talent, of sensual creativity, and the embrace of thousands of loving fans. A glamorous life of beautiful clothes, travel, and love affairs with famous and talented men. She portrayed the pain of letting go of these relationships because in her life, in her career, they just wouldn't work out. But she wouldn't have it any other way. She wouldn't change a thing. It has been her destiny to live this life. And it hasn't been for the faint of heart, for someone without total commitment, for someone not willing to give everything to it. And that has made her a legend, and made me a fan for life." (Tina Winstead)

Many of the stories received focus on Stevie's immense generosity. She inspires artistic talent and provides a release for professional women who just want to be reminded of their inner child and feminine identity.

"I had Stevie on a flight years ago, and I often tell people when they ask who was your nicest celebrity…I tell them, "without a doubt…Stevie Nicks!" She came into the galley to talk with all of us Flight Attendants, and I asked her if she would be willing to write a "little" note to my best friend Angie Diehl who was a lead singer in a band in L.A. and a huge fan of Stevie's. She not only wrote a note…it was a full page letter offering sweet, thoughtful, and encouraging words to my best friend! When I gave it to Angie, she couldn't believe it!" (Rhonda Kraus, Dallas, TX)

"It wasn't until the end of the [Las Vegas] show that my dream came true! A girl that was next to me had an extra meet and greet pass and gave it to me! I practically fell to the floor! When the time came for me to "have my moment in the spotlight", I wouldn't have traded it for the world. I was finally able to walk up to her, shake her hand, and tell her thank you without thousands of screaming fans behind us! That single intimate moment I

will remember forever—her petite frame seeming a mile high, and her delicate handshake that was like a vice-grip.

Meeting Stevie Nicks and telling her thank you and then her saying "No, thank you"—priceless!
What an experience…what a woman!
What other woman in her 50s can still wear six inch platform boots and spin like crazy?

'They call me inspiration…'…this lyric line holds so incredibly true! Inspiration seeps through her pores! I have always been into poetry and writing, but my writing just didn't seem good enough. When I "met" Stevie Nicks, it was like I had my own personal muse! I began writing the most beautiful poetry and songs (some of which have been published)." (Sändor Molnar)

"Most importantly, Stevie has always been an important role model in my life. My brother, Steve, whom I called Stevie since birth until the age of 10, died in 2002 from complications from his kidneys. Steve was in a bad accident during active duty in the National Guard. (The accident was aired on Primetime Live.) He jumped out of a helicopter into Grenada Lake near Memphis, during a training exercise. It left him paralyzed from the neck down. He asked me to sing "Landslide" to him in the hospital many times. He stayed paralyzed for 12 years when he finally died in 2002 on Stevie Nicks's birthday! Stevie inspired my brother and she most definitely inspires me today and always. I love her and I will always remember the child that danced around the house with colors of light bouncing off the walls as I sang song after song, memorizing, and feeling every beat with my soul. Now I sing her songs with pride, while wishing she could only know just how much she truly inspires me." (Tammy Kelly Wroten, Natchez, MS)

"A few years back, I purchased two tickets to see a solo Stevie concert in Camden, NJ. As the date of the show approached, I was able to get a single ticket in the first row. My husband and a friend took the pair of tickets that were located pretty far back in the arena, and I sat alone in my front row seat.

Now, as any die-hard fan knows, Stevie comes to the front of the stage during "Edge of Seventeen" to accept gifts from and shake hands with fans. Through the Enchanted mailing list, I knew that people were planning to bring white roses to hand Stevie during this time. As I was busy getting dressed, I sent my husband out to get my white roses. He brought back a single long-stemmed white rose that had to be at least two feet long, tied with a huge white bow! As "Edge of Seventeen" started, I moved to the front of the stage to give Stevie my rose. Unfortunately, I am pretty short so the stage was above my head. Undaunted I just held up my enormous flower hoping she could reach it. When she got to me, she stopped, took the rose, and mouthed "Thank You" right at me! Needless to say I just about passed out! My husband later told me that all the way in the back he couldn't see me down there, but he saw this big white rose and the huge white bow floating out above the crowd!

After the concert we were telling my mom all about our night and how Stevie took my big flower, and my mom actually started to cry! I asked why, and she said that I am normally so practical and level headed (I'm a doctor) that she couldn't believe that an entertainer could touch me so profoundly. But it's true—Stevie has been my favorite singer for so long, and I've seen her live so many times. Her music reaches people of all kinds and backgrounds, and I think that is just a small part of what makes her so special to her true fans." (Bernadette Mandes Wildemore, M.D., Hatboro, PA)

"First, I want to thank you for offering us Stevie fans the opportunity to be a part of your book. Read between My Lines—I love the title. This in essence defines how Stevie is so intricately and intimately involved and loved by so many devoted fans." (Gayle Rickert)

Thank you Stevie for all that you do. It has been a pleasure writing a book chronicling your musical journey while paying tribute to your many accomplishments.

— Sandy

Stevie with Waddy Wachtel—Performed on the *Today Show*,
September 28, 2005
(Photo by Janet Mayer / Photorazzi)

Endnotes

Introduction

[1] Maggie Gruber, "Paradise Found—An Interview with Stevie Nicks," *Borders.com*, June 2001.

[2] Michael Lyons, "Stevie Nicks: Arizona's Bella Donna Comes Home," *Arizona Living*, September 1983.

[3] Jenny Boyd, *Musicians in Tune* (New York: Simon & Schuster, 1992).

[4] Chris Willman, "Long Distance Winner," *Entertainment Weekly*, May 1, 1998.

Chapter One

[1] Valerie Smaldone, "Spotlight on Stevie Nicks", *WSRS Radio*, Worchester, MA, August 5, 2001.

[2] Nui Te Koha, "Original Rock Chick," *Encore-The Australian Sunday Mail*, February 8, 2004.

[3] Timothy White, "With Her New Solo Album, Fleetwood Mac's Good Fairy Tries to Balance Two Careers," *Billboard*, April 18, 1998.

[4] Jenny Boyd, *Musicians in Tune* (New York: Simon & Schuster, 1992).

[5] Linda Romine, "Emotions Run Deep Between Stevie Nicks and her Dad," *Cox News Service*, 1988.

[6] ibid

[7] Cameron Crowe, "The True Life Confessions of Fleetwood Mac: The Long Hard Drive from British Blues to California Gold," *Rolling Stone*, March 24, 1977.

[8] Keith Olsen, *VH1: Behind the Music: Stevie Nicks*, November 1, 1998.

[9] Brenda Bouw, "First Singer Gave Up Sunbathing, Then Drugs," *The National Post*, May 8, 2001.

[10] Keith Olsen, *VH1: Behind the Music: Stevie Nicks*, November 1, 1998.

[11] David Rensin, "20 Questions: Stevie Nicks," *Playboy Magazine*, July 1982.

Chapter Two

[1] Fred Schruers, "The Lovingest, Fightingest, Druggingest Band of the '70s Comes Back," *Rolling Stone,* October 30, 1997.

[2] Lindsey Buckingham, *VH1: Behind the Music: Stevie Nicks,* November 1, 1998.

[3] Alan Jackson, "Why I had to Marry My Best Friend's Husband," *Woman's Own,* August, 20, 1990.

[4] Courtney Love, "Blonde on Blonde, Interview by Courtney Love," *Spin,* October 1997.

[5] Fred Schruers, "The Lovingest, Fightingest, Druggingest Band of the '70s Comes Back," *Rolling Stone,* October 30, 1997.

[6] Courtney Love, "Blonde on Blonde, Interview by Courtney Love," *Spin,* October 1997.

[7] Dave Forte, "Lindsey Buckingham," *Musician, Listener and Player,* June 1981.

[8] Andrew Means, "A Wild Heart-Stevie Nicks," *The Arizona Republic,* August 18, 1983.

[9] Michael Goldberg, "Stevie Nicks: Back to Mac," *The Record,* February 1982.

[10] Fred Schruers, "The Lovingest, Fightingest, Druggingest Band of the '70s Comes Back," *Rolling Stone,* October 30, 1997.

[11] Howard Cohen, "Stevie Nicks Survives Storms," *The Phoenix Gazette,* June 6, 1994.

[12] Dave Walker, "In Valley, this rock star can go 'slummin around' anonymously," *The Arizona Republic,* August, 12, 1997.

[13] John Grissim, "Big Mac: Two All Gold Albums Special Songs Let-ups Cheesecake Pickles Divorce on a Star-crossed Success Run," *Crawdaddy,* November 1976.

[14] Mark David Hendrickson, "Fleetwood Mac Never Break the Chain, The Rebirth of Fleetwood Mac," *The Music Paper,* June 1990.

[15] Fred Schruers, "The Lovingest, Fightingest, Druggingest Band of the '70s Comes Back," *Rolling Stone,* October 30, 1997.

[16] Alan Jackson, "Why I had to Marry My Best Friend's Husband, *Woman's Own,* August 20, 1990.

[17] Paul Elliott, "Queen of the Stoned Age," *Q Magazine,* May, 2001.

[18] Shawn Sell, "Stevie Nicks Sounding Like a Survivor," *USA Today,* October 16, 1991.

[19] Jancee Dunn, "Stevie Nicks Q&A," *Rolling Stone,* September 22, 1994.

[20] Jim Farber, "New Mac Attack, The Fleetwood crew joins rock's age of reformation," *New York Daily News,* August, 12, 1997.

Chapter Three

[1] Stevie Nicks, "Interviewed by Sarah MacLachlan," *Interview Magazine,* March 1995.

[2] David J. Criblez, "Angel of the Turntable," *The Island Ear,* August 22–September 4, 1994.

[3] Christine McVie, "Talking About Each Other: The Women of Fleetwood Mac," *Glamour Magazine,* September 1987.

[4] Sylvie Simmons, "Stevie Nicks, Macrame Goddess: Confronting the Gates of Elmo," *Creem,* 1982.

[5] Stevie Nicks, "Talking About Each Other: The Women of Fleetwood Mac," *Glamour Magazine,* September 1987.

[6] John Grissim, "Big Mac: Two All Gold Albums Special Songs Let-ups Cheesecake Pickles Divorce on a Star-crossed Success Run," *Crawdaddy,* November 1976.

[7] Stephen Bishop, *Song in the Rough* (New York: St. Martin Press, 1996).

[8] Stevie Nicks, "The Stevie Nicks Story," *The Source: NBC Radio Show,* 1981.

[9] Stevie Nicks, *VH1: Behind the Music: Stevie Nicks,* November 1, 1998.

[10] Stevie Nicks, "The Stevie Nicks Story," *The Source: NBC Radio Show,* 1981.

[11] Red Beard, "*Rumours:* Interview with Stevie Nicks and Mick Fleetwood," *In the Studio,* February 24, 1992.

[12] Lindsey Buckingham, *Classic Albums Fleetwood Mac Rumours,* 1997.

[13] Stevie Nicks and Lindsey Buckingham, *Classic Albums Fleetwood Mac Rumours,* 1997.

[14] Dave Walker, "In Valley, this rock star can go 'slummin around' anonymously," *The Arizona Republic,* August, 12, 1997.

[15] Fred Schruers, "The Lovingest, Fightingest, Druggingest Band of the '70s Comes Back," *Rolling Stone,* October 30, 1997.

[16] Stan Soocher, "That's Not Really Me says Mac's Stevie Nicks," *Circus Weekly,* October 17, 1978.

[17] Liz Derringer, "First Interview Since Fleetwood Mac," *High Times,* March 1982.

[18] Stevie Nicks, *VH1: Behind the Music: Stevie Nicks,* November 1, 1998.

[19] Stevie Nicks, "Rock Singer Tries to Reclaim the Glory Days with her Sixth Solo Release-and a new Outlook," *Miami Herald,* 1994.

[20] Mick Fleetwood, *Classic Albums Fleetwood Mac Rumours,* 1997.

[21] Michael Goldberg, "Stevie Nicks: Back to Mac," *Record*, February 1982.

Chapter Four

[1] Paul Fishkin, *VH1: Behind the Music: Stevie Nicks,* November 1, 1998.

[2] Stan Hyman, "No More Dreaming for Stevie Nicks," *Circus,* December 31, 1981.

[3] Vicky Greenleaf and Stan Hyman, "Stevie Nicks She's Smiling Now," *Rock,* October 1983.

[4] Paul Fishkin, *VH1: Behind the Music: Stevie Nicks,* November 1, 1998.

[5] Liz Derringer, "First Interview Since Fleetwood Mac," *High Times,* March 1982.

[6] Stan Hyman, "No More Dreaming for Stevie Nicks," *Circus,* December 31, 1981.

[7] Blair Jackson, "Stevie Nicks: Poetry in Motion," *Hit Parader,* January 1982.

[8] Stevie Nicks, *Rockline Radio,* Los Angeles, 1981.

[9] Silvie Simmons, "Nicks A Dreamer in the Real World," *Raw,* June 14–27, 1989.

[10] Liz Derringer, "First Interview Since Fleetwood Mac," *High Times,* March 1982.

[11] Blair Jackson, "Stevie-Fleetwood Mac's siren soars with her first solo album *Bella Donna*," *BAM,* September 11, 1981.

[12] David Gans, "Where's Stevie?" *Record,* September 1982.

[13] Liz Derringer, "First Interview Since Fleetwood Mac," *High Times,* March 1982.

[14] Steve Pond, "The Us Interview: Stevie Nicks," *Us,* July 9–23, 1990.

[15] Lance Loud, "Would You stay if she promised you heaven," *Details,* August 1994.

[16] Mick Fleetwood, *VH1: Behind the Music: Stevie Nicks,* November 1, 1998.

Chapter Five

[1] Michael Goldberg, "Stevie Nicks: Back to Mac," *Record,* February 1982.

[2] David Gans, "Where's Stevie?" *Record,* September 1982.

[3] Vicky Greenleaf and Stan Hyman, "Stevie Nicks She's Smiling Now," *Rock,* October 1983.

[4] Blair Jackson, "Stevie Nicks: Poetry in Motion," *Hit Parader,* January 1982.

Chapter Six

[1] Stevie Nicks, *VH1: Behind the Music: Stevie Nicks,* November 1, 1998.

[2] Stevie Nicks, "I Still Love Joe Walsh," *contactmusic.com,* November 27, 2003.

[3] Stevie Nicks, "Innerview with Jim Ladd," KMET Radio Los Angeles, 1986.

[4] Paul Fishkin, *VH1: Behind the Music: Stevie Nicks,* November 1, 1998.

[5] Alan Jackson, "Why I had to Marry My Best Friend's Husband," *Woman's Own,* August 20, 1990.

[6] Roger Catline, "Stevie Nicks drags her heart back to Fleetwood Mac," *The Hartford Courant,* September 14, 1997.

[7] Lesley-Ann Jones, "Stevie Wonder," *You,* June 25, 1989.

[8] James Sevrin, "The Stevie Nicks Experience," Online, 1995.

[9] Stevie Morse, "A Solo Stevie Nicks: Her love affair with music is the one that has lasted," *Boston Globe,* July 14, 1991.

[10] Robin Smith, "In the Nicks of Time," *Record Mirror,* May 20, 1989.

[11] Steve Pond, "The Us Interview: Stevie Nicks," *Us,* July 9–23, 1990.

[12] Lawrence Ferber, "Nicks of Time," *In News Weekly,* May 2, 2001.

[13] Chris Willman, "Long Distance Winner," *Entertainment Weekly,* May 1, 1998.

[14] John Soeder, "A tasty brew of old and new conjures up magic onstage," *Plain Dealer,* July 15, 2001.

[15] Mick Fleetwood, *VH1: Behind the Music: Stevie Nicks,* November 1, 1998.

[16] Robin Smith, "In the Nicks of Time," *Record Mirror,* May 20, 1989.

Chapter Seven

[1] David J. Criblez, "Angel of the Turntable," *The Island Ear,* August 22–September 4, 1994.

[2] Stevie Nicks, "Reflections on The Other Side of the Mirror," By Dan Neer and James Fahey, Westwood One Radio Networks, *Off the Record,* 1989.

[3] Keith Sharp, "Tango: Take Two," *Music Express,* 1989.

Chapter Eight

[1] David J. Criblez, "Angel of the Turntable," *The Island Ear,* August 22–Septembe 4, 1994.

[2] Ryan Murphy, "Q&A," *Us,* August 1994.

[3] Shawn Sell, "Nicks Shedding Gypsy Ways," *USA Today,* August 16, 1994.

[4] David J. Criblez, "Angel of the Turntable," *The Island Ear,* August 22–Sept 4, 1994.

[5] Jancee Dunn, "A Trip to Stevieland," *Harper's Bazaar,* November 1997.

[6] Ray Rogers, "A Storm Called Stevie," *Interview,* July 1998.

[7] Jeff McDonald, "Never Break the Chain," *BAM,* August 22, 1997.

[8] Lindsey Buckingham, *VH1: Behind the Music: Stevie Nicks,* November 1, 1998.

[9] Chris Willman, "The Rebounding Talents of Nicks," *Entertainment Weekly,* May 1, 1998.

Chapter Nine

[1] Steve Morse, "A Solo Stevie Nicks: Her love affair with music is the one that has lasted," *Boston Globe,* July 14, 1991.

[2] David J. Criblez, "Angel of the Turntable," *The Island Ear,* August 22–September 4, 1994.

[3] Lola Ogunnaike, "Electric Lady," *Nylon,* June 2001.

[4] Jeff Johnson, "The Portable Stevie Nicks," *Jane,* June/July 2001.

[5] Chris Willman, "Long Distance Winner," *Entertainment Weekly* (print edition), May 1, 1998.

[6] Lori Perry Nicks, *VH1: Behind the Music: Stevie Nicks,* November 1, 1998.

[7] Chris Willman, "The Rebounding Talents of Nicks," *Entertainment Weekly* (print edition), May 1, 1998.

Chapter Ten

[1] Lawrence Ferber, "Nicks of Time," *In News Weekly,* May 2, 2001.

[2] Barbara Stepko, "Stevie Wonder," *McCalls,* January 1999.

[3] Gary Graff, "Stevie Nicks Says *Shangri-La* Didn't Really Take Seven Years," *aunch,* May 1, 2001.

na Gundersen, "Nicks Reaches Shangri-La," *USA Today,* May 4, 2001.

Graff, "Stevie Nicks Says Shangri-La Didn't Really Take Seven Years," *ay* 1, 2001.

"Queen of the Stoned Age," *Q Magazine,* May 2001.

"Stevie Nicks—Gold Dust Woman Returns, *VH1.com,* April 14,

o Stevie Nicks, solitary romantic has a new album," *New*
01.

mber

Fleetwood Mac," *Performing Songwriter,*

[2] Chris Macias, "Say, they reunited," *The Sacramento Bee,* July 4, 2003.

[3] James McNair, "Return of the Mac," *Independent Review,* April 18, 2003.

[4] ibid

[5] ibid

[6] Dave Walker, "In Valley, this rock star can go 'slummin around' anonymously," *The Arizona Republic,* August, 12, 1997.

[7] James McNair, "Return of the Mac," *Independent Review,* April 18, 2003.

[8] ibid

[9] Jac Chebatoris, "Drama Keeps People Together: Fleetwood Mac's Gold Dust Woman has grown up. A Q&A with Stevie Nicks," *Newsweek,* May 28, 2003.

[10] Stevie Nicks, "Innerview with Jim Ladd," ABC Radio Station Group, *KLOS* Los Angeles, March 21, 2005.

Chapter Twelve

[1] Doug Elfman, "A Vegas Natural," *Las Vegas Review Journal,* May 13, 2005.

[2] Maureen Meyers Farrar, "What Dreams May Come," *Showbiz Weekly (vegas.com),* May 8, 2005.

[3] Jonathan Cohen, "Nicks Making Dreams Come True in Vegas," *Billboard.com,* March 17, 2004.

[4] John Sinkevics, "Stevie Nicks: Says she couldn't feel any luckier right now," *Grand Rapids Press,* June 23, 2005.

[5] Bill Picture, "Gold Dust Woman," *San Francisco Chronicle,* July 24, 2005.

Chapter Thirteen

[1] Stevie Nicks, *VH1: Behind the Music: Stevie Nicks,* November 1, 1998.

[2] Blair Jackson, "Stevie-Fleetwood Mac's siren soars with her first solo album *Bella Donna,*" *BAM,* September 11, 1981.

[3] *RISMedia.com,* "Today's HOME-spun Wisdom," May 26, 2005.

[4] Sylvie Simmons, "Through the Looking Glass Darkly," *Revolution,* November 1989.

[5] Stevie Nicks and Mick Fleetwood, *VH1: Behind the Music: Stevie Nicks,* November 1, 1998.

[6] Blair Jackson, "Stevie-Fleetwood Mac's siren soars with her first solo album *Bella Donna,*" *BAM,* September 11, 1981.

[7] Edna Gundersen, "Nicks Reaches Shangri-La," *USA Today,* May 4, 2001.

[8] Lola Ogunnaike, "Electric Lady," *Nylon*, June 2001.

[9] Doug Elfman, "A Vegas Natural," *Las Vegas Review Journal*, May 13, 2005.

[10] David J. Criblez, "Angel of the Turntable," *The Island Ear*, August 22–September 4, 1994.

Chapter Fourteen

[1] Steve Pond, "The Us Interview: Stevie Nicks," *Us*, July 9–23, 1990.

[2] Guy Blackman, "A magical life," *The Age*, February 12, 2006.

[3] Nui Te Koha, "Original Rock Chick," *Encore-The Australian Sunday Mail*, February 8, 2004.

[4] Steve Morse, "A Solo Stevie Nicks: Her love affair with music is the one that has lasted," *Boston Globe*, July 14, 1991.

[5] Marilyn Beck and Stacy Janel Smith, "The rock 'n' roll gypsy is back with Mac—but don't ask her about grocery shopping," *E! Online*, August 17, 1997.

[6] Jonathan Cohen, "Nicks Making Dreams Come True in Vegas," *Billboard.com*, March 17, 2004.

[7] Lola Ogunnaike, "Electric Lady," *Nylon*, June 2001.

[8] Ritchie Yorke, "Stevie's buzzing," *Queensland Newspaper*, October 30, 2005.

[9] Jim Farber, "Lacing Up Stevie Nicks, solitary romantic has a new album," *New York Daily News*, May 6, 2001.

[10] Guy Blackman, "A magical life," *The Age*, February 12, 2006.

[11] Jim Farber, "Lacing Up Stevie Nicks, solitary romantic has a new album," *New York Daily News*, May 6, 2001.

[12] Mick Fleetwood, *VH1: Behind the Music: Stevie Nicks*, November 1, 1998.

[13] Blair Jackson, "Stevie Nicks: Poetry in Motion," *Hit Parader*, January 1982.

[14] David Wild, "Q&A with Stevie Nicks," *Rolling Stone*, July 5, 2001.

[15] Timothy White, "Stevie Nicks; Long Distance Winner," *Billboard*, April 18, 1998.

Bibliography and Credits

"At Home with Stevie Nicks, Her Desert Oasis." *In Touch Weekly,* September 13, 2004.

"Back in the Nicks of Time." *Sydney Morning Herald,* November 29, 1997.

Beard, Red. *"Fleetwood Mac:* Interview with Stevie Nicks & Mick Fleetwood." By Red Beard. US Album Network Radio Show, *In the Studio,* no. 205 (May 25, 1992).

Beard, Red. *"Rumours:* Interview with Stevie Nicks & Mick Fleetwood." By Red Beard. US Album Network Radio Show, *In the Studio,* no. 192 (February 24, 1992).

Beck, Marilyn and Stacy Janel Smith. "The rock 'n' roll gypsy is back with Mac—but don't ask her about grocery shopping." E! Online, August 17, 1997. *http://www.eonline.com/Celebs/Qa/Nicks/.*

Benson, Joe. *Off the Record.* ABC Radio Station Group, KLOS Los Angeles, September 6, 1997.

Benson, Joe. *Off the Record.* ABC Radio Station Group KLOS Los Angeles, June 2, 1998.

Bishop, Stephen. *Song in the Rough.* New York: St. Martin Press, 1996.

Blackman, Guy. "A magical life." *The Age,* February 12, 2006.

Blehi, Kathy. "Nicks Rocks It With Romance." *USA Today,* April 14, 1986.

Blockbuster Entertainment Awards. FOX, Blockbuster and *Entertainment Weekly* Magazine, April 11, 2001.

Bouw, Brenda. "First Singer Gave Up Sunbathing, Then Drugs." *The National Post,* May 8, 2001.

Boyd, Jenny. *Musicians in Tune.* New York: Simon & Schuster, 1992.

Brogan, Daniel. "One Star Rising, One Falling Cross Paths at Concert." *Chicago Tribune,* June 23, 1986.

Brown, G. "Singer, Colorado soar like birds of a feather." *Denver Post,* August 11, 1991.

Brown, G. "Singer, Younger Crowd Gets Nicks On The Rocks." *Denver Post,* August 11, 1991.

Brown, Mark. "Going your own way easier said than done." *Rocky Mountain News,* July 9, 2004.

Buckingham, Lindsey. *VH1: Behind the Music: Stevie Nicks,* November 1, 1998.

Buckingham, Lindsey. Fleetwood, Mick. Nicks, Stevie. McVie, Christine. McVie, John, *Fleetwood Mac Reunion, "The Dance."* MTV Interview, April 22, 1997.

Cahill, Jeanne A. "A Lesson from the Heart." *Arizona Healthy Living,* July/August 1998.

Carr, Ray and Stevie Clark. *"Rumours."* BBC Radio 2, November 11, 1998.

Catline, Roger. "Stevie Nicks drags her heart back to Fleetwood Mac." *The Hartford Courant,* September 14, 1997.

Chebatoris, Jac. "Drama Keeps People Together: Fleetwood Mac's Gold Dust Woman has grown up. A Q&A with Stevie Nicks." *Newsweek,* May 28, 2003.

Cohen, Howard. "A Wiser Stevie Nicks Builds her New Shangri-La." *Miami Herald,* May 1, 2001.

Cohen, Howard. "Stevie Nicks Survives Storms." *The Phoenix Gazette,* June 6, 1994.

Cohen, Jonathan. "Nicks Making 'Dreams' Come True in Vegas." *Billboard.com,* March 17, 2004.

Coleman, Mark. "Nicks Slips Out of Touch, 'A Review of Rock a Little.'" *Rolling Stone,* Issue no. 466, January 30, 1986.

Connelly, Christopher. "The Second Life of Don Henley." *GQ,* August 1991.

Connelly, Christopher. "Trouble in Fantasyland, Stevie Nicks." *Rolling Stone,* Issue no. 399, July 7, 1983.

Considine, J.D. "For musician Stevie Nicks, creative writing fills a void while she's on tour." *The Baltimore Sun,* July 17, 1991.

Criblez, David J. "Angel of the Turntable." *The Island Ear,* August 22–September 4, 1994.

Crowe, Cameron. "The Photographs: Fleetwood Mac." *Rolling Stone,* Issue 958, September 30, 2004.

Crowe, Cameron. "The True Life Confessions of Fleetwood Mac: The Long Hard Drive from British Blues to California Gold." *Rolling Stone,* Issue no. 235, March 24, 1977.

DeMain, Bill. "War and Peace and Fleetwood Mac." *Performing Songwriter,* Vol. 10, Issue 69, May 2003.

Derringer, Liz. "First Interview Since Fleetwood Mac." *High Times,* March 1982.

DiMartino, Dave. "The Way We Were, Forget Dallas and Dynasty—is the world ready for the Fleetwood Mac reunion?" *Mojo,* September 1, 1997.

Dougherty, Steve and Todd Gold. "High Priestess; Shedding drugs, weight and breast implants, Stevie Nicks whirls back." *People,* January 19, 1998.

Dunn, Jancee. "A Trip to Stevieland." *Harper's Bazaar,* November 1997.

Dunn, Jancee. "Stevie Nicks Q&A." *Rolling Stone,* Issue no. 691, September 22, 1994.

Elfman, Doug. "A Vegas Natural." *Las Vegas Review Journal,* May 13, 2005.

Elfman, Doug. "A Vegas Natural." *Showbiz Weekly,* May 8, 2005.

Elliott, Paul. "Queen of the Stoned Age." *Q magazine,* May 2001.

Farber, Jim. "Lacing Up Stevie Nicks, solitary romantic has a new album." *New York Daily News,* May 6, 2001.

Farber, Jim. "New Mac Attack, The Fleetwood crew joins rock's age of reformation." *New York Daily News,* August 12, 1997.

Farrar, Maureen Meyers. "What Dreams May Come." *Showbiz Weekly* (*vegas.com*), May 8, 2005.

Ferber, Lawrence. "Nicks of Time." *In News Weekly,* May 2, 2001.

Fink, Mitchell. "It Was Fate: Stevie Meets Her Destiny." *New York Daily News Gossip Column,* May 9, 2001.

Fishkin, Paul. *VH1: Behind the Music: Stevie Nicks,* November 1, 1998.

Fleetwood Mac. *Classic Albums Fleetwood Mac Rumours,* David Heffernan. Los Angeles, CA. DVD. BBC, NCRV, VH-1, and Eagle Rock Entertainment for Rhino Home Video, 1997.

Fleetwood Mac, 2001. *Fleetwood Mac Destiny Rules,* Matt Baumann and Kyle Einhorn. New York, NY. DVD. Sanctuary Records Group and Warner Brothers Records/Reprise Records. Candlewood Film, 2004.

Fleetwood Mac. *Fleetwood Mac Documentary and Live Concert,* Tom and Linda Spain, Burbank, CA. VHS and Beta Cassettes. Warner Home Video, 1981.

Fleetwood Mac. *Fleetwood Mac Say You Will, Live in Boston,* Joe Thomas, Burbank, CA. DVD. Reprise Records, WTTW/Chicago, HD Ready, LLC and Soundstage, 2004.

Fleetwood Mac. *Fleetwood Mac Tango in the Night,* Wayne Isham, Burbank, CA. DVD. Warner Reprise Video. A Production of Fleetwood Mac Tours, 2003.

Fleetwood Mac. *Fleetwood Mac The Dance,* Bruce Gower, Burbank, CA. DVD. Warner Reprise Video, 1997.

Fleetwood, Mick and Stephen Davis. "In an excerpt from his upcoming book, Mick Fleetwood tells how 'Rumours' got started." *Rolling Stone,* September 20, 1990.

Fleetwood, Mick. *VH1: Behind the Music: Stevie Nicks,* November 1, 1998.

Fleetwood, Mick with Stephen Davis. *Fleetwood My Life and Adventures in Fleetwood Mac.* New York: William Morrow and Company, Inc., 1990.

Flick, Larry and Melissa Newman. "Rumours." *Billboard,* Vol. 109, Issue no. 33, August 16, 1997.

Flick, Larry. "Stevie Nicks is Ready for 'Trouble,'" *Billboard.com,* December 12, 2001.

Forte, Dave. "Lindsey Buckingham." *Musician Listener and Player,* Issue 33, June 1981.

Gans, David. "Where's Stevie?" *Record,* Volume 1, No. 11, September 1982.

Goldberg, Michael. "Stevie Nicks: Back to Mac." *Record,* February 1982.

Goodman, Mark. "Stevie: Wild Angel On The Wing." *The Faces Interview of the Month,* MTV, Fall 1983.

Graff, Gary. "Sheryl Crow brings life into focus, alongside her music." *Reuters News,* April 16, 1999.

Graff, Gary. "Stevie Nicks on her solo album, the Mac and Tom Petty." *Rolling Stone,* Issue no. 786, May 14, 1998.

Graff, Gary. "Stevie Nicks Says Fleetwood Mac Reunion is a Go." *Launch,* May 2, 2001.

Graff, Gary. "Stevie Nicks Says Shangri-La Didn't Really Take Seven Years." *Launch,* May 1, 2001.

Greenleaf, Vicky and Stan Hyman. "Stevie Nicks She's Smiling Now." *Rock* magazine, October 1983.

Grissim, John. "Big Mac: Two All Gold Albums Special Songs Let-ups Cheesecake Pickles Divorce on a Star-crossed Success Run." *Crawdaddy,* November 1976.

Gruber, Maggie. "Paradise Found—An Interview with Stevie Nicks," *Borders.com,* June 2001.

Gundersen, Edna. "Nicks reaches 'Shangri-La'." *USA Today,* May 4, 2001.

Gundersen, Edna. "Rumours are true: Mac is Back." *USA Today,* August 12, 1997.

Helegar, J. "Talking with Stevie Nicks."*People,* Volume 41, Issue 22, June 13, 1994.

Hendrickson, Mark David. "Fleetwood Mac Never Break the Chain, The Rebirth of Fleetwood Mac." *The Music Paper,* June 1990.

Herbst, Peter. "Mac not hurt by Nicks." *Rolling Stone,* June 29, 1977.

Hinckley, David. "Hall of a Year for Fleetwood Mac." *New York Daily News,* November 30, 1997.

Hyman, Stan. "No More Dreaming for Stevie Nicks." *Circus,* December 31, 1981.

Jackson, Alan. "Why I had to Marry My Best Friend's Husband." *Woman's Own,* August 20, 1990.

Jackson, Blair. "Stevie—Fleetwood Mac's siren soars with her first solo album, *Bella Donna*." *BAM,* September 11, 1981.

Jackson, Blair. "Stevie Nicks: Poetry in Motion." *Hit Parader,* January 1982.

Jerome, Jim. "The Rumors About All Those Fleetwood Mac Splits Were True; And Now Their Comment is Tusk, Tusk." *People,* November 26, 1979.

Johnson, Jeff. "The Portable Stevie Nicks." *Jane,* June/July 2001.

Jones, Lesley-Ann. "Stevie, Wonder." *You,* June 25, 1989.

Katz, Larry. "Sounds Breaking the Chain Solo: Stevie Savors Her New-Found Freedom from Fleetwood Mac." *Boston Herald,* July 17, 1994.

Katz, Susan. *Superwomen of Rock.* New York: Grosset & Dunlap, 1978.

Kenney, Glen. *"Street Angel Review." New York Daily News,* July 17, 1994.

Kessler, Tom. "Not Just Second Hand News." *Dallas Morning News,* April 2, 1993.

Kipnis, Jill. "Henley and Nicks team up for a stop in Clarkston." *The Detroit News,* June 17, 2005.

Lawless, Lucy. "Stevie Nicks' Fajita Round-Up." *Saturday Night Live,* October 17, 1998.

Locey, Bill. "Life of Lindsey; The Former Fleetwood Mac Guitarist is Hitting the Road to Promote His Latest Album, 'Out of the Cradle.'" *Los Angeles Times,* Ventura County Edition, March 4, 1993.

Loud, Lance. "Would You stay if she promised you heaven." *Details,* August 1994.

Love, Courtney. "Blonde on Blonde, Interview by Courtney Love." *Spin,* October 1997.

Lyons, Michael. "Stevie Nicks: Arizona's Bella Donna Comes Home." *Arizona Living,* September 1983.

"Mac Daddy: Reluctant guitarist Lindsey Buckingham on the Mac's big attack." *Rolling Stone,* August 27, 1997. *http://www.rollingstone.com/news/story/_/id/5924429/lindseybuckingham? pageid=rs.ArtistArticles&pageregion =mainRegion.*

Macias, Chris. "Say, they reunited." *The Sacramento Bee,* July 4, 2003.

Manning, Kara. "Recordings—'Street Angel' by Stevie Nicks." *Rolling Stone,* Issue no. 690, September 8, 1994.

Marsh, Dave. "Big Mac: Over 8 Million Sold." *Rolling Stone,* Issue no. 256, January 12, 1978.

Martin, Gavin. "Confessions of a Rock Chick, Stevie Nicks Has Survivied Drink and Drugs to Tour Again with Fleetwood Mac." *Australian Women's Weekly,* March 2004.

McLane, Daisann. "Five Not So Easy Pieces, Fleetwood Mac is more than the sum of its parts." *Rolling Stone,* Issue no. 310, February 7, 1980.

McDonald, Jeff. "Never Break the Chain." *BAM,* Issue 516, August 22, 1997.

McNair, James. "Return of The Mac." *Independent Review,* April 18, 2003.

Means, Andrew. "A Wild Heart—Stevie Nicks." *Arizona Republic,* August 18, 1983.

Meldrum, Ian "Molly." *The Meldrum Tapes, Interview.* ABC and MTV, 1986.

Moret, Jim. Interview with Stevie Nicks. *CNN Showbiz Weekly,* May 2, 1998.

Morse, Stevie. "All Crow Wants to do is Rock." *Boston Globe,* April 9, 1999.

Morse, Stevie. "A Solo Stevie Nicks: Her love affair with music is the one that has lasted." *Boston Globe,* July 14, 1991.

MTV FANatic, with Elena Bernal, August 20, 1998.

Murphy, Ryan. "Q&A," *Us,* August 1994.

Nelson, Steffie. "Stevie Nicks-Gold Dust Woman Returns." *VH1.com,* April 14, 2001.

Nicks, Jess. *Arizona Heart Institute Press Release,* July 20, 2005.

Nicks, Lori Perry. *VH1: Behind the Music: Stevie Nicks,* November 1, 1998.

Nicks, Stevie and Christine McVie. "Talking About Each Other: The Women of Fleetwood Mac." *Glamour Magazine,* September 1987.

Nicks, Stevie and Lindsey Buckingham Interview. "Buckingham and Nicks: Heart to Heart." *Microsoft Music Central.* August 1997.

Nicks, Stevie. "Innerview with Jim Ladd." ABC Radio Station Group, KLOS Radio Los Angeles, March 21, 2005.

Nicks, Stevie. "Innerview with Jim Ladd." KMET Radio Los Angeles, 1986.

Nicks, Stevie. "Innerview with Jim Ladd." KMET Radio Los Angeles,1979.

Nicks, Stevie. "Interview with Stevie Nicks." Rockline Radio, Los Angeles, 1981.

Nicks, Stevie. Interviewed by David Letterman. *David Letterman Show,* June 16, 1998.

Nicks, Stevie. Interviewed by Jay Leno. *Tonight Show with Jay Leno,* April 30, 1998.

Nicks, Stevie. Interviewed by Rosie O'Donnell. *Rosie O'Donnell Show,* May 3, 2001.

Nicks, Stevie. Interviewed by Sarah McLachlan. *Interview* magazine, March 1995.

Nicks, Stevie. Interviewed by Sheryl Crow. *Interview* magazine, May 2001.

Nicks, Stevie. "Off the Record." Interview by Mary Turner. ABC Radio Station Group, KLOS Los Angeles, 1986.

Nicks, Stevie. "Off the Record." Interview by Mary Turner. ABC Radio Station Group, KLOS Los Angeles, December 1994.

Nicks, Stevie. "*Reflections on The Other Side of the Mirror.*" By Dan Neer and James Fahey. Westwood One Radio Networks, *Off the Record* (promotion interview), 1989.

Nicks, Stevie. *Rock Hour* Radio Interview. Tommy Vance. *BBC,* 1991.

Nicks, Stevie. *Rock Hour* Radio Interview. Tommy Vance. *BBC,* October 1984.

Nicks, Stevie. *Stevie Nicks in Concert.* CBS FOX Video Music. Welsh Witch Productions, Ltd., 1982.

Nicks, Stevie. *Stevie Nicks Live at Red Rocks,* Marty Callner, Chatsworth, CA. VHS and DVD Lightyear Entertainment, L.P, 1987, 1995.

Nicks, Stevie. "The Stevie Nicks Story." *The Source:* NBC Radio Show, 1981.

Nicks, Stevie. *Timespace The Best of Stevie Nicks* (liner notes). Modern Records, 1991.

Nicks, Stevie. *VH1: Behind the Music: Stevie Nicks,* November 1, 1998.

Nui Te Koha. "Original Rock Chick." *Encore—The Australian Sunday Mail,* February 8, 2004.

Nui Te Koha. "Sex, Drugs and Stevie Nicks." *Courier Mail,* September 27, 2003.

Nui Te Koha. "Nicks knocks Madge's pash." *Herald Sun,* September 19, 2003.

Ogunnaike, Lola. "Electric Lady." *Nylon,* June 2001.

Olsen, Keith. *VH1: Behind the Music: Stevie Nicks,* November 1, 1998.

Orf, Chris Hansen. "Jess Nicks, father of Fleetwood Mac's dies." *East Valley Tribune,* August 16, 2005.

Pacheco, Javier. "The Penguin Q&A Sessions," July 5–24, 1999. *http://www.fleetwoodmac.net/penguin/qa/javierpacheco_photo_67.htm.*

Parade Sunday Newspaper Magazine, December 15, 1991.

Picture, Bill. "Gold Dust Woman." *San Francisco Chronicle,* July 24, 2005.

Pond, Steve. "The Us Interview: Stevie Nicks." *Us,* July 9–23, 1990.

Pond, Steve. "Stevie Nicks Twirling in Her Fantasy World." *Los Angeles Times,* October 4, 1983.

Raub, Kevin. "Stevie Nicks Sued by Investor." *Allstar News*, June 3, 1999.

Reavy, Pat. "Fleetwood Mac Returning to S.L." *Deseret Morning News*, August 1, 2003.

Rensin, David. "20 Questions: Stevie Nicks." *Playboy*, Volume 29, Number 7, July 1982.

"Reprise's Stevie Nicks Returns With Crow In Tow." *Billboard*, February, 17, 2001.

RISMedia.com Today's HOME-Spun Wisdom, May 26, 2005. *http://www. rismedia.com/index.php/article/articleview/10451/1/1/.*

Rogers, Ray. "A Storm Called Stevie." *Interview*, July 1998.

Romine, Linda. "Emotion Runs Deep Between Stevie Nicks and her Dad." *Cox News Service*, 1988.

Rosen, John N. *Direct Psychoanalytics Psychiatry.* New York: Grune & Stratton, 1962.

Schruers, Fred. "The Lovingest Fightingest Druggingest Band of the '70s Comes Back." *Rolling Stone*, Issue no. 772, October 30, 1997.

Secher, Andrew. "Fleetwood Mac: The Model 1970s Band." *Hard Rock*, Vol. 1, No. 3, September 1978.

Sell, Shawn. "Nicks Shedding Gypsy Ways." *USA Today*, August 16, 1994.

Sell, Shawn. "Stevie Nicks Sounding Like a Survivor." *USA Today*, October 16, 1991.

Selvin, Joel. "Shoreline Steals Show From Nicks." *San Francisco Chronicle*, July 16, 1986.

Sevrin, James. The Stevie Nicks Experience. *Online*, 1995.

Sharp, Keith. "Tango: Take Two." *Music Express*, Volume 13, Issue 134, 1989.

Sheffield, Rob. "Review of Enchanted: The Work of Stevie Nicks." *Rolling Stone*, Issue no. 786, May 14, 1998.

Simmons, Sylvie. "Nicks A Dreamer in the Real World." *Raw*, no. 21, June 14–27, 1989.

Simmons, Sylvie. "Through the Looking Glass Darkly." *Revolution*, November 1989.

Simmons, Sylvie. "Stevie Nicks, Macrame Goddess: Confronting the Gates of Elmo." *Creem*, 1982.

Sinkevics, John. "Stevie Nicks: Says she couldn't feel any luckier right now." *Grand Rapids Press,* June 23, 2005.

Smaldone, Valerie. *"Spotlight on Stevie Nicks."* WSRS Worcester, MA, August 5, 2001.

Smith, Aidan. "I fight like a dog every day." *Scotsman.com* News, November 2, 2003. *http://scotlandonsunday.scotsman.com/thereview.cfm ?id=1207982003.*

Smith, Robin. "In the Nicks of Time." *Record Mirror,* May 20, 1989.

Soeder, John. "A tasty brew of old and new conjures up magic onstage." *Plain Dealer,* July 15, 2001.

Soocher, Stan. "That's Not Really Me says Mac's Stevie Nicks." *Circus Weekly,* October 17, 1978.

"Starsound Special." RKO Radio Neworks, Los Angeles, December 21, 1981.

"Stars Over the Derby—A Fleetwood Mac reunion will top a stellar Derby celebrity lineup." *Courier-Journal,* April 16, 1996.

Stepko, Barbara. "Stevie Wonder." *McCalls,* January 1999.

"Stevie Nicks: Going Her Own Way." myLAUNCH Q&A, April 30, 1998.

"Stevie Nicks: I Still Love Joe Walsh." *Contactmusic.com,* November 27, 2003. *http://www.contactmusic.com/new/xmlfeed.nsf/mndwebpages/stevie %20nicks.%20i%20still%20love%20joe%20walsh.*

"Stevie Nicks, Paul Fishkin, Mick Fleetwood, Lori Nicks, Keith Olsen. Narrator: Jim Forbes. *"VH1 : Behind the Music,* William Harper and Paulina Williams, New York, NY. Sony Music Studios, November 1, 1998.

"Stevie Nicks." *VH1 : Storytellers,* Michael Simon, New York, NY. Sony Music Studios, November 1, 1998.

"Stevie Nicks: Rock Singer Tries to Reclaim the Glory Days with her Sixth Solo Release—and a new Outlook." *Miami Herald,* 1994.

Sullivan, Caroline. "The Witch is Back." *The Guardian,* February 12, 1998.

Sutcliffe, Phil. "Take it to the Limit." *Mojo,* December 2003.

Swenson, John. "Rumours Review" *Rolling Stone,* Issue no. 237, April 21, 1977.

"The Church of Stevie Nicks". Capitol Hill Blue, *News of the Weird,* December 29, 1998.

"The Heart of Stevie." *Scottsdale Life,* July/August 2000.

Tuck, Stephanie. "Stevie Nicks: Desert Rose." *In Style,* March 2002.

vanHorn, Teri. "Stevie Nicks to Make 'Trouble' Across North America." *VH1.com,* May 15, 2001. *http://www.vh1.com/artists/news/1443733/05152001/nicks_stevie.jhtml.*

vanHorn, Teri. "Stevie Nicks' Shangri-La Bring Together Old and New." *VH1.com,* April 23, 2001. *http://www.vh1.com/artists/news/1443047/04232001/nicks_stevie.jhtml.*

Vare, Ethlie Ann and Ed Ochs. *Everything you want to know about Stevie Nicks.* New York: Ballantine Books, 1985.

Walker, Dave. "In Valley, this rock star can go 'slummin around' anonymously." *Arizona Republic,* August 12, 1997.

Walters, Charley. *Headliners: Fleetwood Mac.* New York: Grosset & Dunlap, 1979.

Warner Brothers Records/Reprise Records. *Trouble in Shangri-La,* press kit, 2001.

Wheeler, Steven P. "Since she first exploded on the rock scene in 1975 as the seductive focal point of Fleetwood Mac, Stevie Nicks has been as much an enigma as a consistent platinum-selling act." *Music Connection,* Volume 18, No. 15, July 1994.

White, Timothy. "Stevie Nicks; Long Distance Winner." *Billboard,* April 18, 1998.

White, Timothy. "With Her New Solo Album, Fleetwood Mac's Good Fairy Tries to Balance Two Careers—and Two Personalities." *Rolling Stone,* Issue no. 351, September 3, 1981.

Wild, David. "Q&A with Stevie Nicks." *Rolling Stone,* Issue no. 872, July 5, 2001.

Willman, Chris. "Crystal' Mesh Sheryl Crow and Stevie Nicks invite EW to their first recording session." Entertainment Weekly Online, October 26, 1998.

Willman, Chris. "Long Distance Winner." *Entertainment Weekly* (print edition), May 1, 1998.

Willman, Chris. "The Rebounding Talents of Nicks." *Entertainment Weekly* (print edition), May 1, 1998.

Yahoo! Music. Associated Press. "Nicks' Landslide Wins BMI Song Award."
  November 6, 2003. *http://music.yahoo.com/read/news/12175854.*
Yorke, Ritchie. "Stevie's buzzing." *Queensland Newspaper,* October 30, 2005.

www.catanna.com/steviephotos.htm.
www.inherownwords.com C. Kilger.
www.nicksfix.com Stevie Nicks, John Kinney.
Buckingham, Cory. "Tour Diaries." *http://www.stevie-nicks.info/index.php*
?option=search&searchword=tour+diaries June 7, 2004.
Buckingham, Cory. "Tour Diaries." *http://www.stevie-nicks.info/index.php*
?option=search&searchword=tour+diaries May 30, 2004.
Buckingham, Cory. "Tour Diaries." *http://www.stevie-nicks.info/index.php*
?option=search&searchword=tour+diaries May 25, 2004.
Buckingham, Cory. "Tour Diaries." *http://www.stevie-nicks.info/index.php*
?option=search&searchword=tour+diaries March 9, 2004.

Stevie Nicks Discography

Buckingham Nicks
Polydor Records 1973
Produced by Keith Olsen

Bella Donna
Modern Records 1981
Produced by Jimmy Iovine and Tom Petty

The Wild Heart
Modern Records 1983
Produced by Jimmy Iovine

Rock A Little
Modern Records 1985
Produced by Stevie Nicks, Rick Nowels, Jimmy Iovine, Mike Campbell, Keith Olsen, and Chas Sandford

The Other Side of the Mirror
Modern Records 1989
Produced by Rupert Hine

Timespace: The Best of Stevie Nicks
Modern Records 1991
Produced by Danny Kortchmar, Jon Bon Jovi, Jimmy Iovine, Tom Petty, Rupert Hine, Bret Michaels, Rick Nowels, Chas Sandford, Michael Campbell, Chris Lord-Alge, and Stevie Nicks

Street Angel
Atlantic Recording Corporation 1994
Produced by Thom Panunzio, Stevie Nicks, and Glen Parrish

The Enchanted Works of Stevie Nicks (3 CD Box Set)
Atlantic Recording Corporation 1998
Produced by Lindsey Buckingham, Mike Campbell, Rupert Hine, Jimmy
Iovine, Bob James, Chris Lord-Alge, Stevie Nicks, Rick Nowels, Keith
Olsen, Thom Panunzio, Gordon Perry, Chas Sandford, Andrew Slater,
John Stewart, and Don Was

The Divine Stevie Nicks
Divine (Netherlands) 2000

Trouble in Shangri-La
Reprise Records 2001
Produced by Stevie Nicks, Sheryl Crow, John Shanks, Mike Campbell, Jeff
Trott, David Kahne, Rick Nowels, and Pierre Marchand

Planets of the Universe
Reprise Records 2001
Produced by John Shanks and Stevie Nicks

Fleetwood Mac Discography
(with Stevie Nicks)

Fleetwood Mac
Warner Bros. Records Inc. 1975
Produced by Fleetwood Mac and Keith Olsen

Fleetwood Mac—Re-mastered
Warner Bros. Records Inc. 2004
Produced by Fleetwood Mac, David McLees, and Gary Peterson

Rumours
Warner Bros. Records Inc. 1977
Produced by Fleetwood Mac, Richard Dashut, and Ken Caillat

Rumours—Re-mastered
Warner Bros. Records Inc. 2004
Produced by Fleetwood Mac, David McLees, and Gary Peterson

Tusk
Warner Bros. Records Inc. 1979
Produced by Fleetwood Mac (Special Thanks to Lindsey Buckingham), Ken Caillat, and Richard Dashut

Tusk—Re-mastered
Warner Bros. Records Inc. 2004
Produced by Fleetwood Mac, David McLees, and Gary Peterson

Fleetwood Mac Live
Warner Bros. Records Inc. 1980
Produced by Ken Caillat, Richard Dashut and, Fleetwood Mac

Mirage
Warner Bros. Records Inc. 1982
Produced by Lindsey Buckingham, Richard Dashut, Ken Caillat, and, Fleetwood Mac

Tango in the Night
Warner Bros. Records Inc. 1987
Produced by Lindsey Buckingham and Richard Dashut

Fleetwood Mac's Greatest Hits
Warner Bros. Records Inc. 1988
Produced by Fleetwood Mac, Keith Olsen, Richard Dashut, Ken Caillat, Lindsey Buckingham, and Greg Ladanyi

Behind the Mask
Warner Bros. Records Inc. 1990
Produced by Greg Ladanyi and Fleetwood Mac

The Chain (4 CD Box Set)
Warner Brothers Records (Australia) 1992
Produced by Fleetwood Mac, Lindsey Buckingham, Keith Olsen, Richard Dashut, and Ken Caillat

25 Years—Selections from The Chain (2 CD Box Set)
Reprise Records 1992
Produced by Fleetwood Mac, Lindsey Buckingham, Keith Olsen, Richard Dashut, and Ken Caillat

The Dance
Reprise Records 1997
Produced by Lindsey Buckingham and Elliot Scheiner

The Very Best of Fleetwood Mac
Reprise Records 2002
Produced by Fleetwood Mac, Lindsey Buckingham, Keith Olsen, Richard Dashut, and Ken Caillat

Say You Will
Reprise Records 2003
Produced by Lindsey Buckingham, John Shanks, and Rob Cavallo